CW00740197

Made with L♡VE by locals

Didi & Co is the first guidebook co-created by local insiders for fellow urban explorers. Places, pictures and pointers are all handpicked and generated collaboratively. Enjoy the best of Paris, brought to you by our cream-of-the-crop local experts. Take their word on all things fresh in the city; they are the cool kids you can trust.

Curious to spot hidden gems along your heritage walks? Want to find that one cute neighbourhood café where you'll feel home, pronto? Eager to know where the groovy party is? Fancy tasting the local food scene's top finds? Didi & Co has got you covered with authentic haunts and secret spots. Join the community; let Didi & Co be your go-to guide to explore in style.

@didiandcotravel   www.didiandcotravel.com

our STORY

Didi & Co was born the day two sisters started putting together pointers about their home cities - Paris, Bombay and Sydney - for visiting buddies and newcomers. The endeavour continued on the road with compiling tips from friends across the world, and resulted in a community of like-minded travellers and cool insiders.

The two globetrotters decided to design their own funky travel guidebook as an offbeat alternative to the plain existing options they didn't identify with. Too mainstream or too niche, too backpacker or too luxurious, not creative enough.

Traveling together taught them to master the art of compromise so they usually find a middle ground between authentic and trendy, affordable and comfortable.

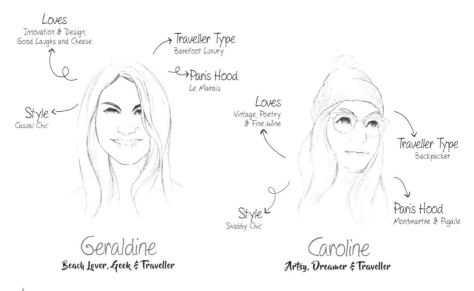

Loves
Innovation & Design,
Good Laughs and Cheese

Traveller Type
Barefoot Luxury

Paris Hood
Le Marais

Style
Casual Chic

Loves
Vintage, Poetry
& Fine Wine

Traveller Type
Backpacker

Style
Shabby Chic

Paris Hood
Montmartre & Pigalle

Geraldine
Beach Lover, Geek & Traveller

Caroline
Artsy, Dreamer & Traveller

In this digital age, we bet on old school with print over app.
Simply because we believe some of us still like to unplug our phones
when travelling and enjoy keeping a tangible trace of places visited on
our bookshelf.

You're still wondering who this Didi is?
Well, see: in Hindi, 'didi' means 'sister' but extends to anyone you
consider with respect and affection. Those who you decide to call as
such are your go-to people. We want Didi & Co to be your go-to guide so
you feel home away from home.

Explore and experience. Wander and wonder.
Connect with others; reconnect with yourself.
Take time to pause and feel the city.
Create memories.

Happy travels,
Caroline Didi & Geraldine Didi

Contents

in a nutshell

Boasting of an eternal emotional appeal, Paris enthrals and enchants. It drips with history, art, and charm. Monuments and museums are part of the city's mystique, and will transport you, but Paris also holds a lesser-known, modern and multicultural facet.

Behind the picturesque petite bistros, cobblestone streets and gardens *à la française,* breathes a mosaic of cultures and communities. Be it fashion or food, the tradition lives up to its reputation, but the contemporary reality is just as fun to discover!

Rather than the City of Love or the City of Lights, it's first and foremost the City of Life that cultivates a self-indulgent *art de vivre.* Stroll its villages, hills, canals, hidden nooks and crannies. Eat, drink, dance, and rub shoulders with the Parisians: they're less snooty than what the legend goes!

NITTY-GRITTY

2.2M
LIVING SOULS IN
PARIS
67M IN FRANCE

EMERGENCY CALL
15

58KG THAT'S HOW MUCH BAGUETTE A
FRENCH EATS EVERY YEAR

SPEND IN
€UROS

1-20
ARRON-
DISSEMENTS

=

**PARISIAN
DISTRICTS**

**THE WEST IS MORE BOURGY,
THE EAST MORE EDGY**

(TOSSED BUT
NOT SUNK)
PARIS RESILIENT
MOTTO

GETTING AROUND

€10   €50

€1.90/SINGLE
€7.50/DAY

MOBILIS = DAILY/WEEKLY PASS

DOWNLOAD THE 'NEXT STOP PARIS' APP
ONLINE ROUTES AND OFFLINE MAP
TO HELP YOU NAVIGATE THE METRO.

 PAY-AND-GO BIKES
DAILY/WEEKLY PASSES

MONEY TALK

 €6

 €6

 €3

 €7

LOCAL LINGO

APÉRO // SHORT FOR "APÉRITIF"

BOBO // BOURGEOIS + BOHÈME = HIPSTER

BOULANGERIE // BAKERY

BISTRO // INTIMATE, LOW-KEY EATERY
SERVING A HOMEY FARE

BISTRONOMIE // BISTROT + GASTRONOMIE
= FINE FARE IN A CASUAL BISTRO VIBE

CARAFE D'EAU //
PICHER OF COMPLIMENTARY TAP WATER

CAVE À MANGER // WINE SHOP MEET DELI BAR

CHARCUTERIE // COLD CUTS: CURED OR
COOKED HAMS, «SAUCISSON» (CURED SAUSAGE)...

FROMAGE(RIE) // CHEESE (SHOP)

GUINGUETTE // NO-FUSS JOINT BY THE WATER

PÉTANQUE // THE NATIONAL SPORT

PLANCHE // PLATTER
(OF CHEESE AND/OR CHARCUTERIE)

QUARTIER // HOOD

SUR PLACE / À EMPORTER // EAT-IN / TAKE-AWAY

(MIS)UNDERSTANDINGS ?

LUNCH BREAKS ARE SACRED > FOLLOW
THE FOOD CLOCK (12-2PM, 7-10PM)

SUNDAYS ARE TOO! TIME STANDS
STILL AND SHOPS SHUT

MEALS ARE A TREAT SO WE MAKE THEM
LAST: SIT BACK, CHILL, CHAT, LINGER!

APÉRITIF IS A MUST - EVENING WINE AND
NIBBLES ARE A SOCIAL AFFAIR

PARISIAN SERVICE IS A BIT ALOOF,
DON'T TAKE OFFENSE!

A "CAFÉ" IS AN EXPRESSO SHOT
WANT MILK? ASK FOR A "CAFÉ CRÈME"

TOURIST VISA

- EU PASSPORTS: NO VISA NEEDED

- US, CAN, AUS, NZ, JPN, SG, MY: NO VISA
NEEDED FOR A SHORT STAY —UP TO
3 MONTHS— IN THE SCHENGEN AREA.

- OTHER PASSPORTS: SCHENGEN VISA,
UP TO 3 MONTHS (€60)

PARIS MUSEUM PASS

PLANNING A LOT OF SIGHTSEEING?
THIS HASSLE-FREE PASS GIVES YOU
DIRECT ACCESS TO MOST MAJOR
MONUMENTS AND MUSEUMS.

2-6 DAYS FROM €48

EN.PARISMUSEUMPASS.COM

Instagram Folks
TO FOLLOW

1. mylittleparis
2. durevie
3. doitin_paris
4. lefooding
5. linstantparisien
6. lostncheeseland
7. frenchwords
8. basicfrenchwords_
9. parisianivores
10. time_out_paris
11. lebonbon
12. quefaireaparis
13. parisjetaime
14. seemyparis

DURE VIE

BE A REAL
PARISIENNE
or die trying

Book
lover

Je t'aime plus
que la pizza
I love you more than pizza

Soyon
Fous

Bucket List

1

Hop on a bike, or embark one of those cute retro cars for a city tour in style

@paris_authentic

2

Share a *planche* (meat and cheese platter) while sipping wine for the *'apéro'* at a bistro terrace

3

Play pétanque by the canals

4

Browse the *'bouquinistes'* (used book stalls) along the banks of the Seine to pick up an old French edition

5

Munch on a crêpe or an ice-cream, strolling the paved streets of the Cité Island

6

Explore the covered passages. Galerie Colbert, Vivienne or Véro-Dodat, Passage des Panoramas, du Grand Cerf, des Princes, Verdeau or Jouffroy...the 2nd district is full of them!

7

Spend a with the *étoiles* night for a ballet at the Opéra Garnier

8

Pack a baguette, a stack of cheese and a bottle of wine, and head to a park for a picnic

9

Rent your own electrical boat to see the city with fresh eyes (see p.116)

@marindeaudoucefrance

10

Rise above on *'La Butte'*, walk the cobblestone streets and soak in Montmartre bohemian charm

Paris
City Map

1 MOULIN ROUGE

2 SACRÉ-COEUR

3 OPÉRA

4 LOUVRE

5 NOTRE-DAME

6 MUSÉE D'ORSAY

7 TOUR EIFFEL

8 ARC DE TRIOMPHE

8

BOIS DE
BOULOGNE
FOREST

TROCADÉRO

PALAIS DE
TOKYO

7

SEINE RIVER

MONTPARNA
TOWER

14

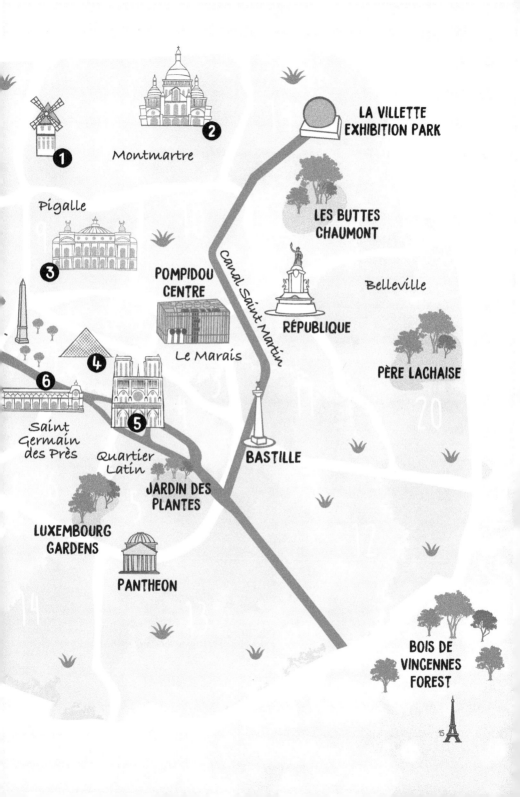

1 Montmartre

2

LA VILLETTE
EXHIBITION PARK

Pigalle

LES BUTTES
CHAUMONT

3

POMPIDOU
CENTRE

Canal Saint Martin

RÉPUBLIQUE

Belleville

Le Marais

4

PÈRE LACHAISE

6

5

Saint
Germain
des Prés

Quartier
Latin

JARDIN DES
PLANTES

BASTILLE

LUXEMBOURG
GARDENS

PANTHEON

BOIS DE
VINCENNES
FOREST

15

@vm.photoparis @lebonmarcherivegauche

Saint-Germain-des-Prés

Montparnasse & the Latin Quarter

Arts & Art de vivre

An aura surrounds this village in the trail of Notre-Dame. Once the hotspot for the intelligentsia, it has retained the essence of Parisian flair - timeless sophistication and a dash of culture. From the 1920's to the 60's, jazz clubs were pulsating and its legendary cafés were literary hangouts. Philosophers, New-Wave filmmakers and artists made it their haven. Today, book and antique shops, art galleries, publishing houses and indie theatres remain, joined by charming bistros, lively bars and designer boutiques. The adjacent Saint-Michel will lead you to the depths of the Latin Quarter. With institutions such as the Sorbonne and Beaux-Arts, it's the heart of academic life. A little less chic but no less exciting!

MUSÉE CARNAVALET
© François Grunberg

Le Marais

Old meet new

Favoured ever since medieval times, this central place is where the king set up his private pad and noblemen lived in lavish hôtels particuliers. Traditionally Jewish, LGBT at heart, and hip on the edges, the multifaceted Marais is a bit of all this, yet somehow hasn't lost its identity. It's first the historic "Vieux Paris" whose maze of cobbled streets brims with old-world charm and architecture of all eras. An art hub, it's filled with galleries and museums housed in private mansions. Designer boutiques and vintage stores make it a prime spot for shopping. A hive bustling with activity, it also offers quiet nooks and hidden courtyard gardens. As for the Haut-Marais (Upper-Marais), it's where the hype is, with its lot of trendy stores and eateries.

Bastille / Oberkampf
A moveable feast

Bordered by the République and Bastille squares, squeezed between the Marais and Ménilmontant, this neighbourhood spreading across the 10th and 11th districts is a buzzing hipster hive. Boasting a brilliant bar culture, this lively stretch is a night-owl playground packed with concert venues, cheap and festive bars. It also bursts with creative eateries, cool coffeeshops and modern gourmet spots (notably bakeries). Heading north towards the picturesque canal Saint-Martin will immerse you in a rather arty and alternative vibe. Here, the food becomes more veg-friendly and gluten-free, but nonetheless exciting. Quaysides and bylanes are dotted with trendy canteens and sustainable shops.

Montmartre & Pigalle
La bohème...

Even before Amélie immortalized it, Montmartre was the postcard Paris one always dreamt of! Despite its touristy quirks, it's an enchanting place. Behind the visible tip of the Sacré-Coeur, breathes a bucolic oasis overlooking Paris: La Butte ("the hill"). Its vineyards and winding cobbled lanes ooze poetry and the charm of a bygone bohemian time. Down the hill, Pigalle lures the eye with its Moulin Rouge and cabarets. It's an aging lady of the night, who's gone a facelift. Keeping its core festive spirit in place, while getting rid of the sleaze, the revamped "SoPi" is now the place to be. If kinky shops are still well off on the boulevard de Clichy, the more respectable South-Pigalle offers trendy bars, contemporary canteens and gournmet shops. The cute rue des Martyrs especially is foodie heaven with an irresistible village vibe!

The West

Glitzy and ritzy

The Concorde plaza marks the start with a bang of the chic western part of Paris. With a bang, for it opens with no less than the "most beautiful avenue in the world": the prestigious Champs Elysées. The "wealthy West" then spreads on both sides, across the 7th, 8th, 16th and 17th districts, around large Haussmanian boulevards that radiate from the Arc de Triomphe. Here, extravagance rubs shoulders with discrete bourgeois refinement. Mostly residential and pretty quiet, it's rather a destination for a nature break in the Bois de Boulogne forest. The most notable point of interest is the Trocadéro Square and its breathtaking view of the lit-up Eiffel Tower.

Le Sentier & Les Grands Boulevards

Work hard, play harder

Traditional home of the textile industry, the gentrifying Sentier fills with start-ups and digital agencies, though a few ready-to-wear fashion stores hold on. With the nearby Bourse (stock exchange), this locale stays pretty business-oriented, but head east for some afterwork fun! The Montorgueil pedestrian street is a haven of gourmet shops, including institutions that resisted the passing of time.

Running from the Opéra to the République, these Grands Boulevards are dotted with bars, clubs, brasseries, heaps of theatres and live music venues. This historic district, nestled a stone's throw from the Louvre, also holds architectural gems: elegant Haussmanian buildings and the notable covered passages that are a joy to discover!

© Marc Bertrand : Paris Tourist Office

@vm.photoparis

© Amélie Dupont - Paris Tourist Office

Belleville / Ménilmontant
Arty & Alternative

Playfully nicknamed "Babelville" for the melting pot that makes up its population – a variety of communities from successive waves of immigration, Belleville might be a little different from the Paris you pictured but it's a sweet surprise! Here, Chinese and Vietnamese joints hobnob with halal and kosher butchers, and a multitude of exotic grocery stores. Multicultural yet quintessentially Parisian, Belleville is a working-class suburb full of character. Remote in the eastern heights and perched atop a hill, these two quaint districts are their own little village that exudes a rustic *joie de vivre*. Their narrow cobblestone streets unveil street art, artist studios and friendly neighbourhoods bars.

© Gavroche Père & Fils

Barbès, Jaurès & the Northeast

At the feet of Montmartre, the seedy Barbès and Goutte d'Or hoods are a colourful mosaic crawling with people. These city edges first welcomed small-town workers in furnished hostels. Turned homebase of all European and African immigrants, it's now an eclectic ethnic mix. Streets here breath of Cameroon and Senegal, stocking wax fabrics, spices and exotic grocers. Not going to lie, you might still see some shady business under the aerial métro station, but the place is now more respectable after the urban revamp! Off Gare du Nord, sprawls rue du Faubourg St-Denis, a pool of saree shops and Indian joints. These are mostly residential spots but, in case you like to go off the beaten tracks, they offer excellent eats and underground parties. La Villette, at the eastern tip, is a cool cultural playground.

Slices Of Paris

From The Bookshelf

1 **Everything (or Almost Everything) About Paris**
By: Jean-Christophe Napias

This Bible of all things Parisian is a witty collection of fun and random facts, backstories, lists, quotes and more, which is sure way to shine at dinner parties. A pleasant read, it casually offers cultural insights and a whiff of that Parisian *je-ne-sais-quoi*.

2 **The Only Street in Paris: Life on the Rue des Martyrs**
By: Elaine Sciolino

The homage of an American in Paris (New York Times correspondent E. Sciolino) to the vibrant Parisian street life. Celebrating the little things, the neighbourhood's colourful residents and their incredible stories, this charming ballad is an ode to a soulful Paris that has endured through time.

3 **Metronome: A History of Paris from the Underground Up**
By: Lorànt Deutsch

Lorànt Deutsch is this one friend who always has an anecdote to share. The actor has been entertaining the French for years with his passion for history, racy and vivid storytelling. In Metronome, he tells the story of the capital through 21 subway stops. A fun way to discover the hidden treasures of the city.

The Paris Playlist

VAPEURS D'ÉQUATEUR Syracuse *Acid-Pop*	06:55	**CHALEUR** Bamao Yendé *Afro-House*	05:55
CANOPÉE Polo & Pan *Electro-Pop*	04:37	**AFRO TRAP PART 3 (CHAMPION'S LEAGUE)** MHD *Rap*	02:34
VANILLE FRAISE L'Impératrice *Disco-Pop*	04:15	**SAYARAT 303** Acid Arab *Afro-House*	06:02
THIS WAY Aleqs Notal *House*	07:03	**LA MALINCHE** Feu! Chatterton *Rock*	04:12
PARIS CITY JAZZ Bellaire *Deep-House*	05:46	**FÊTE DE TROP** Eddy de Pretto *Rap / Chanson*	02:50
NIGHT Bambounou *Techno*	04:45	**L'AMOUR EN SOLITAIRE** Juliette Armanet *Chanson*	02:56

didiandco   https://play.spotify.com/user/didiandco

On Big Screen

Before Sunset by Richard Linklater   Year: 2004

They met in Vienna, reunite in Paris. The sequel to acclaimed indie romance Before Sunrise brings Celine and Jesse back together. They met by chance, clicked in a unique way, spent the night getting to know each other and decided to meet again six months later. While wandering Parisian streets, they resume the conversation started nine years ago. Thanks to uninterrupted takes and brilliant dialogues, the film feels oh-so-real. In a delicate dance, they unfold details about their lives, give answers, and ask more questions. They make one believe in second chances.

Spots on Screen: La Coulée Verte, Shakespeare & Co, Marais, Île St-Louis.

Two Days in Paris by Julie Delpy   Year: 2007

Two lovers, a Paris getaway... nope, this is not the romantic comedy you'd expect! No accordion ballads, picture-perfect sunsets or fancy dinners. Trust indie icon Julie Delpy (the heroine of the Before trilogy) to be a tad subtler for her directional debut! Instead, on the menu are exes, upset stomachs, irritating habits, awkward anecdotes, cultural misunderstandings and French oddities. The film follows Franco-American couple Marion and Jack on their Paris stopover. Juggling clichés and relationships dynamics, this flick is a joy to watch.

Spots on Screen: Canal Saint-Martin, Père Lachaise cemetery.

Holy Motors by Leos Carax   Year: 2012

« *Weird, weird, that's so weird!* »: this line, uttered by a man in Holy Motors could sum up the whole work of Carax, the enfant terrible of French cinema; and all the more this film, which follows the journey of a mysterious man named Monsieur Oscar. He travels Paris from dawn to dusk, wearing many masks, playing many roles, within a bigger and more obscure picture. Visually stunning and beautifully weird, Holy Motors is, by turns, exhilarating and seriously unsettling.

Spots on Screen: Père Lachaise cemetery, La Samaritaine department store.

Midnight in Paris by Woody Allen   Year: 2011

Be it New York, Rome or Barcelona, Allen masters love letters to cities. This dreamy journey into the Parisian art scene of the 1920s is no exception. It transports you a time when Hemingway, Fitzgerald, Man Ray and other American legends were living it up in Paris. That vibrant era is brought back by the daydreaming hero, Gil. Through his walkabouts, he will meet a clutch of characters played by a stellar cast, the crème de la crème of French cinema. A must for all Paris lovers, and those who believe in magic.

Spots on Screen: Giverny, Versailles, Musée Rodin, Le Meurice Palace...

Made in Paris

Funky local stuff to bring home

A FASHION ICON, THE SQUARE SILK SCARF GOT FUNKIER. TIED IN THE HAIR, AS A TOP OR A JEWEL, IT'S A PARISIAN MUST!

HERMÈS CARRÉ FROM €360

THE ULTIMATE FRENCH PIECE. THIS CULT MISCHIEVOUS KIDS WEAR BRAND DOES TIMELESS PRACTICAL BASICS FOR GROWN-UP KIDDIES, 0 TO 936 MONTHS

PETIT BATEAU SAILOR SHIRT FROM €39

A SOLID BASIC, THE ELEGANT AND SIMPLE DESIGN WILL ADD A DASH OF FRENCH CASUAL CHIC TO YOUR WARDROBE. IF YOU'RE A PARISIAN AT HEART, SAY IT IN STYLE!

Parisien

SWEAT 'PARISIEN' BY MAISON KITSUNÉ FROM €150

THESE COUTURE CHOCO BARS ARE WRAPPED IN FUNKY AND FUN PAPERS. TASTING AS GOOD AS IT LOOKS, THE CHOCOLATE IS ARTISAN, LOCAL, NATURAL.

LE CHOCOLAT DES FRANÇAIS FROM €5.50

22

YOUR VERY OWN ARTWORK, THIS DIY MAP WILL DELIGHT THE (NOT-SO-) LITTLE ONES. A SUPER SOUVENIR OR TRAVEL INSPIRATION!

OMY COLOURING POSTER FROM €19

ORIGINAL UNDIES 100% MADE IN FRANCE: TRADITIONAL KNOW-HOW IN THE SERVICE OF MODERN-DAY SWAG. FOR LADIES TOO.

LE SLIP FRANCAIS UNDIES FROM €29

UNIQUE JEWELLERY, HANDCRAFTED JUST FOR YOU. BECAUSE WORDS AND A WIRE ARE ENOUGH TO MAKE YOU FEEL SPECIAL.

ATELIER PAULIN JEWELLERY FROM €95

THE NATURAL FRAGRANCES BY LEGENDARY PERFUMER WILL FILL YOUR HOME WITH A TOUCH OF SAINT-GERMAIN SOPHISTICATION.

DIPTYQUE SCENTED CANDLES FROM €26

23

Secret Spots for a Stellar Vista

CAFÉ DE L'HOMME

17, place du Trocadéro (16th) Ⓜ Trocadéro

🅾 @cafedelhomme

For a ringside seat to feast your eyes upon the Eiffel Tower, this is it! Bang in front of it, the terrace of this legendary building is the closest and clearest view you'll get of it. The menu's pricey, so save it for an occasion. Best come here for coffee or an evening drink.

🕐 Mon-Sun 12pm-2am ☎ +33 1 44 05 30 15

CAFÉ GEORGES

Centre Pompidou 6th floor (4th) Ⓜ Rambuteau / Hôtel de Ville

🅾 @centrepompidou

Café Georges is one place to impress. Sprawled across the sixth floor of the Pompidou Centre, it boasts a design that's literally a slice of modern art. Needless to say, the view from above the tubes is wow. It's not cheap, so keep this for a special indulgence.

🕐 Wed-Mon 12pm-2am ☎ +33 1 44 78 47 99
Closed on Tue

MONSIEUR BLEU

20, avenue de New York (16th) Ⓜ Trocadéro

🅾 @monsieur_bleu

A stylish space with an Art-Deco touch, this restaurant within the Palais de Tokyo boasts elegant interiors and fantastic food, not to mention a terrace with an unrivalled view of the Eiffel Tower.

🕐 Mon-Sun 12pm-2am (service till 11pm)

☎ +33 1 47 20 90 47

TERRASS HOTEL

12-14, rue Joseph de Maistre (18th) Ⓜ Abbesses

🅾 @terrasshotel

Weekend brunch, evening drink or panoramic lunch... as many occasions to come chill on the terrace of the aptly named Terrass Hotel. It's a green zone with sofas and sunbeds. Laidback vibe, decently priced menu and wonderful views all guarantee sweet times!

☎ +33 1 44 92 34 14

24

MONTPARNASSE TOWER
33, avenue du Maine (15th) Ⓜ Montparnasse
📷 @montparnasse_observation_deck   Ⓢ €18

The only inner-city skyscraper, the Montparnasse tower offers a dizzying 360-degree view over the whole city. Rise 200 meters above street level and admire every bit of Paris, in daylight or after dark, from the most central lookout point.

SACRÉ-COEUR DOME
35, rue du Chevalier de la Barre (18th) Ⓜ Abbesses

The highest lookout point in Paris! The climb is not for the faint-hearted (300 steps) but you'll get rewarded with Paris in all its glory, sprawling at your feet.

 Mon-Sun 9:30am-8pm (5pm in winter)   Ⓢ €6

INSTITUT DU MONDE ARABE
IMA 1, rue des Fossés Saint-Bernard (5th) Ⓜ Jussieu
📷 @institutdumondearabe

Sitting on the banks of the Seine, the Institute of the Arab World (see p.37) looks straight over Notre-Dame and the two islands. What's super sweet, its rooftop is free-access!

 Tue-Sun 10am-6pm   Ⓢ Free
Thu & Sat 10am-9pm / Closed on Mon

LE PRINTEMPS
Le Printemps Maison, 9th floor 64, bd Haussmann (9th)
Ⓜ Havre-Caumartin / Auber

Offering a panoramic vista over Parisian roofs, the Opera and the Eiffel Tower, the rooftop of the famous department store Le Printemps is a great refuge for a snack break between shopping binges, and your cheapest option for a drink with a view.

 Mon-Sat 9:35am-8pm (8:45pm on Thu) / Sun 11am-7pm

PARC DE BELLEVILLE
47, Rue des Couronnes (20th)
Ⓜ Couronnes

A green spot set on the heights of the Belleville hill, this park overlooks the city and offers an open view from a distance. Close enough to see the Eiffel Tower twinkle, but detached so you have a fresh perspective!

 Mon-Fri 8am-5:45pm   Ⓢ Free
Sat-Sun 9am-5:45pm

VICTOR
© Renaud Cambuzat

SOLÈNE

MARIE

GIULIETTA

NICHOLLE

ALICIA

MEET THE LOCALS

Renaud Cambuzat

VICTOR LUGGER

@ @bigmammagroup

He's got the Italians' bonhomie, their warmth and volubility. But at heart Victor is French, first and foremost. His stomach can't pick a side, really… For two years now, his "sexy squadra" (a clutch of young Italian chefs) have been wafting freshness and happy vibes on the Parisian food scene. With his pal Tigrane Seydoux, he is the maestro of a triumphant symphony: the Big Mamma company (a group of top-notch trattorias).

Don't be misled by that preppy look or the elite B-school resume; Victor spends more time trawling markets and tiny Tuscany villages than inside his CEO digs. He speaks Italian like one, goes hunting foodstuff at the farmers' market, knows how to make his own pasta and roast coffee…. Challenges are his raison d'être, but what excites him the most is life, its simple, honest pleasures. That is how this foodie took the great leap, dropping the reins of a successful start-up to return to the basics. A devotee of high-class products, he dived right in, hitting the Italian roads to source the best stuff straight from the artisans – butchers, market gardeners, cheese-makers and wineries.

NOTABLE FEATURE

He is an aficionado of Italian culture in all its forms, be it music, lifestyle, art, and of course wine and food!

YOU'RE LIKELY TO FIND HIM…

on gourmet walkabouts at the **Aligre market,** in the 11th (see p.75)

FAVOURITE HAUNTS

Aux Deux Amis (see p.98) is where he hangs out for drinks with his gang, also for the fab food and vibrant vibe. A fan of **Café Oberkampf** (see p.66) brunch, his fine dining go-to guys are **Le Baratin** and **Sauvage** (see p.50 & 52)

VICTOR'S TIP

"Get up early and have a crap coffee in a beautiful brasserie, with the papers. Rent a bike and ride through the 11th, 10th and 9th. Oh, and do check out the local markets…the very soul of the city."

Jérôme Galland

Joann Pai

NOTABLE FEATURE

Don't call her cat lady yet, but she is the proud parent of the cutest grumpy cat!

YOU'RE LIKELY TO FIND HER...

in her cellar in Montmartre or at an indie rock gig at **La Mécanique Ondulatoire** (see p.93). In her spare time, this epicurean scouts the city's bylanes, on the lookout for cool, new spots to eat and drink.

FAVOURITE HAUNTS

If she isn't throwing wine-and-dine parties for her cork dork gang, her home base is **VIGNES** (see p.99), a natural wine bar helmed by friends. For lunch, her favourite hangout would be the cosy **Café de l'Industrie** (see p.54), and for dinner her last love is **Hero** (see p.60), a cool Korean with killer cocktails.

SOLÈNE MIROGLIO

[O] @solene_mcqueen

If the world of wine sounds obscure and uptight, meet Solène. She'll change your mind! With her, PDOs* turn into poetry, the sophisticated loosens up and the abstruse becomes crystal clear. From her mop of copper hair to the cherry lips, red defines her to a T; she embodies its sensuality and passion. Her personality is the subtle blend of strength and softness that makes for exceptional red vintages.

This rock-fan diva personifies a new generation of wine experts, unabashed, emancipated, and oozing personality. Their approach is more natural, if casual. Turned wine selector somewhat belatedly (she was a midwife in her previous avatar), Solène now pilots a funky cellar shop where you pair your wine with your evening's mood: Netflix, soccer, ladies night or barbecue. In due time, she'll have her own wine bar, in Paris or maybe abroad since she's also bitten by the travel bug.

* PDO = Protected Designations of Origin

SOLÈNE'S TIP

In Montmartre, don't stay only in the touristy enclave around the Sacré Cœur. Come check out Les Abbesses. It's only two streets on, just as cute, and so much more authentic!

MARIE MAUTALEN

She has something of young Jane Birkin, the child-like legend of the 60's. Same pencil-thin silhouette and retro bangs. Same sweet little face, timid grin, dreamy eyes and modest mood. Marie is the modern-day Parisian icon girl. Her effortless elegance is made of timeless basics (a trench, a perfecto). For her, true luxury lies in simplicity and material quality. Mixing sneakers and bombers with designer pieces, she rejuvenates the French fashion etiquette.

After years of modelling, she became her own creative director. On her fashion blog, Into Your Closet, she composes looks with her most exciting finds – mostly French. Her agenda is filled with shootings and collections previews, yet, the one thing she would not miss for anything is the end of school day. And when she takes her glamour shoes off, Marie is first and foremost a loving mummy to Louise (8) and Léonard (4). This it-mum has made home a district that mirrors her discrete refinement, the 1rst arrondissement. A hyper-central pad handy for this busy bee, who can change clothes up to four times a day. She can swing by whenever, and adjust outfits to schedule or weather.

NOTABLE FEATURE

Regardless of her delicate birdie vibes, Marie is a serious sport junkie! She runs, swims, attends a badass cycling class, practises yoga, tennis, canoe and what not. Motherhood never got in the way of her working out (she even drove a sporty stroller to keep running with Baby!)

YOU'RE LIKELY TO FIND HER...

shooting in the streets, gardens, and bistros: Paris is her playground! The Palais Royal Gardens especially, just a short hop from her home, are her go-to place, be it for a work lunch a walk with the fam'.

FAVOURITE HAUNTS

She's a fan of **Season's** healthy brunch options (see p.62). The cool **Fish Club** is her hangout for dinner, and **Le Fumoir** her cosy boudoir for a cocktail or a coffee.

MARIE'S TIP

"Walk, walk, walk and lose your way! That's how you discover the most charming spots!"

PIU PIU A.K.A GIULIETTA CANZANI MORA

📷 @piu_piu_

"Piu Piu" is French for the sound that birds make, and this bubbly avatar perfectly conveys the upbeat energy that Giulietta radiates. As a DJ, producer, curator, radio host and vocalist, this multifaceted lady keeps the beat going. Her groovy sound breathes of Detroit and Chicago, as she's a huge fan of house (from garage to ghetto). With the Girls Girls Girls crew, she has been shaking up the Parisian scene, putting more chicks behind the decks. She has also been a part of the indie web radio Rinse France since the early days with her residency 'Grooveboxx', which travels to clubs regularly for fun dance parties.

Giulietta grew up between the 5th and 13th districts – read in an Amélie-scenic part of Paris, meets dead quiet Chinatown, meets ghetto skater spots. That's probably why she is in her element in all sorts of vibes! Today, her hood is Strasbourg St-Denis with a foot in the hip Marais and the other in the dive 10th. It's perfect for her, as she is a person who loves all things random. She bumps into mates and lets herself be carried away by the wind.

She's got exciting stuff in the pipeline – the first release of her label Grooveboxx to start with! Parties, of course, solo and with her Rinse bros. She's also concocting a series of podcasts: the KINDMUNITY, a lab for creative folks finding ways to make this world a better place.

NOTABLE FEATURE

Her exotic name comes from Uruguay, where her father is from. A star multi-instrumentalist, he gave her the music bug, bringing her up on a diet of percussions and psychedelic beats in his own in-house studio.

YOU'RE LIKELY TO FIND HER...

partying here and there on weekdays; it all depends on the line-up, really, but **La Station** (see p.108) and **Le Palace** are her special dance spots. Saturdays are made for recovery brunch with her gang! But her absolute fave is a romantic dinner at the acclaimed **Clamato** on Sundays.

FAVOURITE HAUNTS

For a drink, she's a fan of the select **Hôtel Bourbon**, lair of the night-owls. This foodie also loves intimate places that make you feel home. Caring about the staff and vibe just as much as the eats, she's the loyal type! Her second homes count the gastro-pub **Martin Boire et Manger**, as well as **Vivant** (see p.50). Her daily hangouts are **Echo** (see p.69) and the vegan-friendly **Wild & the Moon**.

GUILIETTA'S TIP

"There isn't just "one" Paris but dozens, and that's what's killer! The best way to really see Paris is to do many random things and to meet all the different communities who make things happen in this city!"

NICHOLLE
KOBI

@nichollekobi

Picture the Parisian girl. Slender, natural, effortlessly elegant... and white. Paris doesn't run out of modern muses (Charlotte Gainsbourg, Caroline de Maigret, Jeanne Damas...), but they all convey the same archetypal image. Nicholle started to draw simply because she couldn't identify with what she saw. Painting women in fifty shades of black and brown, this Frenchie from Congolese origin redesigns a more realistic portrait of the Parisienne.

Her art brings out a black femininity that's oh-so-refreshing! Enhancing curvy silhouettes and nappy hair, it's an ode to diversity and pride. Nicholle's world is urban and glamour, sprinkled with self-love words. Her inspiring illustrations come in a series of girly goodies (makeup pouches, tote bags, tees). But those feel-good vibes are also joined by more political pieces (Don't Shoot), which made her Black Women's Art a hit in the U.S.

After exhibiting through American cities, she is now touring Europe. Off to a promising start, her (yet-secret) new projects will take her back to America, where she will open a second studio.

NOTABLE FEATURE

She had to give up art to pay her bills, but thankfully, being pregnant allowed her to get back to drawing. A fashion enthusiast, she got inspired by Garance Doré. She put her sketches out there via Instagram, and so began the social media success-story.

YOU'RE LIKELY TO FIND HER...

munching on Asian eats rue Beaubourg. This street in the 3rd district holds the best little joints in town! For some family time, this mum of three likes lounging in the parks, especially the cute **Batignolles Square**.

FAVOURITE HAUNTS

For a drink or a coffee, she's got a soft spot for **Klay Saint Sauveur**, in Montorgueil. This beautiful tropical joint transports you to American country-clubs and their retro-chic feel. This fan of Asian food favours the 10th district, especially the excellent **Street Bangkok** (see p.60).

NICHOLLE'S TIP

"Don't be afraid to go out of the touristy tracks! Paris is full of surprises; around every corner awaits a different vibe and crowd. Don't be shy; people are always cordial. Rent a flat or get a homestay – you must see the typical Parisian homes. Plus, the morning bakery run is part of the fun!"

ALICIA TRÉGUER

📷 @foodloverparis

Everything in Alicia's life is driven by the mantra: live life to the fullest. Indulgence is her religion. She seeks beauty in all its forms, be it gourmet food, sleek deco objects or dazzling travels. But don't you think she's a fancy-schmancy babe: it doesn't take Michelin stars, designer spas or exotic trips to far-flung countries to make her happy.

Happiness can also be a baguette and cheese on a trek to Normandy. It's all in the way you view things, really. And Alicia can see beauty in the mundane! She savours and celebrates the simple joys. This epicurean delights in sharing her finds and faves with a community of connected foodies.

Her secret dream? Her own café in Paris, although the concept remains her secret for now. In the meantime, she combines her wanderlust with that geek streak of hers, in a job that fits like a glove; she handles social media for a big hotel brand.

NOTABLE FEATURE

She is a true blue Parisian, born and raised here, but it's the South of France that rules her heart (a Provence summer house, her window to the blue sky).

YOU'RE LIKELY TO FIND HER...

bargain hunting in the Marais or visiting city nooks to discover new food gems.

FAVOURITE HAUNTS

She has a soft spot for **Peonies**, a healthy café-florist, and their flower-based pastries. For world food, she loves **Nanashi** and their beautiful bentos (see p.61). She's also a big fan of the **Big Mamma** venues (see p.49), of their killer cocktails, stunning setting, the adorable Italian staff and their super products sourced straight from Italy.

ALICIA'S TIP

*"Swing by the Seine. Whether it's for an impromptu picnic on the banks or a few drinks on a barge -**Monsieur Mouche, Rosa Bonheur**. The laid back ambience, pretty view, oasis far from the madding traffic... a dream place in the sun!"*

EXPLORE

HERITAGE LANDMARKS

EIFFEL TOWER
Place du Trocadéro Trocadéro

The iconic "Iron Lady" towers over Seine River, with a benevolent eye on Paris. If you're up to the climb, it's better to pre-book tickets so you can cut through the queues. But if you don't have the patience for queuing and €25 to spare, even a distance-view is awe-inspiring. More spectacular, to be honest. The best spot for that is the Trocadéro Square, where you can admire it head to toe. And mind you don't miss the sparkle when the tower switches to disco mode for five minutes every hour after sunset: sheer magic!

🕐 Mon-Sun 9am-12am

@arjunradhakrishnan

MUSÉE D'ORSAY
1, rue de la Légion d'Honneur (7th) Assemblée Nationale

This one-of-a-kind museum takes residence in an old railway station; it's worth a visit, for the Beaux-Arts building is itself a work of art! Statues and paintings have replaced the former platforms and tracks. Don't miss the monumental clock ticking over the Seine, with the city as backdrop. Home to the Impressionists, this museum shows such iconic artworks as Monet's 'Water Lilies'. Orsay is your best bet if you must pick just one museum, and feel too lazy for the overwhelming grandeur and timelines of the Louvre.

🕐 Tue-Sun 9:30am-6pm (till 9:45pm on Thu)   💲 €12
    Closed on Mon

LE LOUVRE
Rue Rivoli (1st) (M) Palais Royal Musée du Louvre

The world's largest art museum can get a little intimidating, but the mystique atmosphere is irresistible, especially when day turns into night and the glass pyramid lights up. Skip the visit if you're in town just for a short while. Instead, the Tuileries Gardens, sprawling off the Louvre, draw you in for a stroll. Don't miss the royal perspective of the 'historical axis'. Starting from the pyramid heading to the Concorde obelisk, then the Champs Elysées Arc de Triomphe and beyond, up to the modern Arche de la Défense, it's just one straight line, all eight kilometres!

🎟 **Museum:** Tue-Mon 9am-6pm / Wed & Fri till 9:45pm
Closed on Tue

SACRÉ-COEUR
35, rue du Chevalier de la Barre (18th) (M) Anvers

You'll have to climb some way to ascend to the immaculate basilica (Feel lazy? Take the cable car), but it's all worth it, since what you'll get is one of the most panoramic views over Paris. The Sacred Heart church stands veritably atop the town – its white dome the highest lookout point. The square is always filled with folksy busker melodies, a foretaste of bohemian Montmartre, which starts right here in the narrow cobblestones leading off behind the church.

$ Dome climb €6

🎟 Climb: Mon-Sun 8:30am-8pm (summer)
9am-5pm (winter)

NOTRE-DAME
Parvis Jean Paul II (4th) (M) St-Michel - Notre-Dame

Anyone who has read Victor Hugo has a picture of this cathedral imprinted on their souls. And the Gothic masterpiece doesn't disappoint. Inside, the stained-glass windows are exquisite, even gravity defying. Get up on the towers for a breath-taking, panoramic view. Linger among the gargoyles, protecting the grand old dame in her dramatic serenity. Gush over the delicate lines carved into their faces; awesome!

💡 **Extra Tip:** To avoid the long queues at the towers, download the savvy app Jefile and choose a preferred time.

🎟 Climb: 10am-6:30pm (summer, till 11pm Fri-Sat in July-Aug)
10am-5:30pm (winter)

$ Towers climb €10

OPÉRA GARNIER
8, rue Scribe (9th) (M) Opéra

Dance-lover, history or architecture buff, you'll be glad you dropped by. Right up, the Parisian opera house is a feast for the eyes. What a magnificent building! If the grand staircase, rows of chandeliers and the Marc Chagall ceiling don't make your head spin, the atmosphere will. The enchanting place is filled with legends and mysteries. Take the guided tour, and if you can score a ticket for a performance, yay ! It's all the more magic.

🎟 Mon-Sun 10am-5pm $ €11

HIDDEN URBAN GEMS

MUSÉE JACQUEMART ANDRÉ
158, boulevard Haussman (8th) (M) Miromesnil

(O) @jacquemartandre

Looking for bits of Versailles and the Louvre rolled into one? Minus the aching legs? This private mansion is that secret spot you were dreaming of! Lesser-known but still remarkable, the museum brings together architecture and art. The collection, wide and varied, focuses on Italian Renaissance. Not an art buff? The mansion is stunning, boasting refined furniture and a long list of delights: winter garden, monumental stairways, private apartments and ceremonial rooms. It was the residence of André, a collector, and his wife Nélie Jacquemart, a renowned artist. They travelled the world to acquire rare pieces, which replaced children for these two art lovers.

(K) Mon-Sun 10am-6pm (till 8.30pm on Mon)

(C) +33 1 45 62 11 59   (S) €13.50

LE PAVILLON DES CANAUX
39, quai de la Loire (19th) (M) Laumière

(O) @lepavillondescanaux

Along the Canal de l'Ourcq stands a one-of-a-kind house replete with secrets. Once the residence of the head of the Parisian waterways, the building was abandoned for years before being done up for its second coming as a community hangout. « As homey as it gets » is the watchword here. The house set-up has been retained, so you can still have tea in the bedrooms, chill in the bathtub or slice and dice on the kitchen table. Explore, make yourself at home! This wonder of a venue serves as coffee shop, co-working space and much more, since they host a series of events (healthy, DIY, activist, kids…)

(K) Mon-Wed 10am-12am / Thu-Sat 10am-1am / Sun 10am-10pm

(C) +33 1 73 71 82 90

PLACE DES VOSGES
(4th) Ⓜ Saint-Paul

Around a street, almost randomly you stumble upon this majestic red-brick structure, with its myriad arcades and geometric symmetry. It's a sheltered frame of serenity, nestled just off the bustling Bastille and the Marais. The oldest planned square in the city (early 17th century), this plaza retains much of its original look and tranquillity. Ensconced amidst a series of terraced houses (homes of the upper bourgeoisie during the monarchy), the Louis XIII gardens take centre stage. Stroll along the alleys or take a breather in the lawn... it's a lovely place to people watch!

GALERIE VIVIENNE
5, rue de la Banque (2nd) Ⓜ Bourse

Paris is filled with charming covered passages, but Galerie Vivienne is a favourite. Is it the colourful mosaic floor? Or sunlight pouring through that large glass-roof? Then maybe it is the boutiques that somehow kept their quaint charm. We're not quite sure, but the arcade, built in 1823 and superbly maintained, will wow you. Wandering along wooden storefronts – even if it's just for window-shopping (the options are pretty high-end) – always transports you into a space untouched by time. Check out the delightful antique bookshop (Librairie Jousseaume)!

Ⓚ Mon-Sun 8:30am-8:30pm

BUREN'S COLUMNS
Palais Royal (1st) Ⓜ Palais Royal Musée du Louvre

Just like the pyramid at the Louvre, these candy-striped columns raised quite a few eyebrows in 1986 when they came up in the courtyard of the Palais Royal. They still do. Not everyone's a fan of the contemporary interrupting the historic. Conceptual artist Daniel Buren plays precisely on this, questioning the link between an artwork and its setting to measure the impact of space on perception.

Today, most Parisians have adopted it as a strolling spot and playground. The installation bears Buren's trademark stripes, marking 260 pillars of various sizes. Titled Les Deux Plateaux (Two Levels), there's also an underground portion. And don't miss the palace garden!

HIDDEN URBAN GEMS

MUSÉE DE MONTMARTRE & JARDINS RENOIR
12-14, rue Cortot (18th) Ⓜ Anvers / Abesses
📷 @museemontmartre

On top of the hill, overlooking the vineyards and the city, this house – the oldest in Montmartre – is way more than a museum! With artists' studios and hidden gardens, it's a charming place to take a peek at this quaint slice of bohemian history. In its heyday, they were all here, living, loving, creating: Auguste Renoir, Toulouse-Lautrec, Modigliani, Utrillo. Their art is all over the walls, here. Dive into the history of Montmartre, its arty angst and infamous cabarets. Or lounge in the Renoir gardens, if you prefer.

🎟 Mon-Sun 10am-6pm (7pm in summer)   📞 +33 1 49 25 89 39   💲 €9.50

SHAKESPEARE & CO
37, rue de la Bûcherie (5th) Ⓜ Saint-Michel - Notre-Dame
📷 @shakespeareandcoparis

Opposite Notre-Dame, sitting on the banks of the Seine, this green storefront is the stuff of legend. Founded in 1951 by American George Whitman, the iconic English-language bookshop was the hangout of the expat writing dream team of the time (Joyce, Hemingway, Stein, Fitzgerald...), and home to the anglophone arty community. The 17th-century building is packed to the rafters with books. Explore its nooks and crannies, where you'll find mementos, manifestos and poetic quotes. These walls drip bohemian. There's a café, a cat, buskers and regular events.

🎟 Mon-Sun 10am-10pm   📞 +33 1 43 25 40 93

© Gavroche Père & Fils

CATACOMBS

1 avenue du Colonel Henri Rol-Tanguy (14)
Ⓜ Denfert-Rochereau

Ⓞ @museecarnavalet

This hidden gem really takes the cake, since it's buried not six, but sixty-five feet under the ground! One of its kind, this amazing underground spot will give you the chills while teaching you Parisian history at the same time. Did you know that, in 1785, cemeteries were packed, so we started burying Parisians in this maze of unused tunnels that run under the city? Yep. So millions of skeletons, no less. Dive into the mysterious innards of the City of Lights and explore its darker, freakier, lesser-known side. You must get fast passes: don't waste time in the endless queue. Book on catacombes.paris.fr

Ⓧ Tue-Sun 10am-8:30pm / Closed on Mon

Ⓢ €13 / Fastpass €29 / Free for kids

@amauryzep

PALAIS DES ÉTUDES, ÉCOLE DES BEAUX-ARTS

14, rue Bonaparte (6th) Ⓜ Saint-Germain des Près

Ⓞ @beauxartsparis

The building of the School of Fine Arts (les Beaux-Arts) hides a room that only those in the know visit. This open courtyard was covered with a glass roof in 1860 to welcome statue casts and sculpture pieces given by the Louvre for art students to practice. Blending classic and modern inspirations (Roman-inspired columns, but also metal and sandstone), it's a bi-colour curiosity. Open only when the school has exhibitions.

Ⓧ Tue-Sun 1pm-7pm

Ⓒ +33 1 47 03 50 00

RUE DE CRÉMIEUX

(12th) Ⓜ Bastille

Tucked away in an unassuming part of town lies the most colourful street in Paris! For a change, no Haussmannian grandeur involved, only a rather rustic charm. This tiny, cobblestoned stretch is a rainbow of pastel façades that remind of Portobello. Originally a working-class estate, it's now a slice of the countryside within city-centre limits, much loved by cats and bloggers. The alleyway is all serendipity (trompe l'oeil, plants and painted details to be spot), so keep an eye open and enjoy the picturesque walk down rainbow row!

EAT

GRUB ON THE GO -FINE FAST FOOD-

MERSEA

6, rue du Faubourg Montmartre (9th)
Ⓜ Grands Boulevards
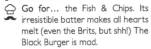 @merseaparis

Not only does the name play the Frenglish card, the cuisine too is a matter of fusion, since it's the French take on an English classic: fish and chips. Creative recipes, a superfine fish (pollack, from sustainable fishing), and a tartare sauce to die for... this is what happens when a Michelin-awarded chef decides to honour his Breton origins and give fish street-food a gourmet twist.

🍽 Go for... the Fish & Chips. Its irresistible batter makes all hearts melt (even the Brits, but shh!) The Black Burger is mad.

⏱ Mon-Sun 11:30am-11pm

📞 +33 9 73 22 46 13

💲 Dive

© Didier Adam

BIG FERNAND

40, place du marché Saint-Honoré (1st)
Ⓜ Pyramides
& Montorgueil, Montparnasse,
Poissonnière, Galeries Lafayette, BHV
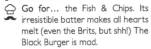 @big_fernand

In the land where fine cooking reigns and fast food was heresy for long, meet the Hamburgé! This gourmet burger brings together street-foodies and purists who never compromise on quality. The French touch comes not only from cheese, obviously (cheddar gets swapped with blue cheese or Cantal), but also from the dressing. Exit nasty ketchup, bonjour homemade sauces! The meat is local, the bread artisanal, the (oh-so-French) fries freshly hand-cut — all top quality. Oh, and the burgers are named after French men; so, you'll have to choose between Lucien and Paulin. Too picky? You can create your own.

⏱ Mon-Sun 12pm-10:30pm
    Sat 12pm-11pm

📞 +33 1 81 63 08 63

💲 Dive

GRUB ON THE GO -FINE FAST FOOD-

PNY (PARIS NEW-YORK)
24, rue Pierre Fontaine (9th) Ⓜ Pigalle
& Marais, Oberkampf, Faubourg St-Denis

Ⓞ @pnyburger

Exceptional French matured beef for American-inspired burgers, washed down with craft beers, in cool company. Funky deco and funkier tunes to boot.

🍴 Go for... the meaty and cheesy Smoky Blue or the avocado-loaded Morning California

🎯 Mon-Sun 12pm-3pm & 7pm-11:30pm 📞 +33 1 48 74 91 70 💲 Casual Chic

BLEND
4, rue de l'Ancienne Comédie (6th) Ⓜ Odéon
& Marais, Sentier, République, Bastille

Ⓞ @blend

Crafted with buttery brioche buns baked in-house and the finest meat from a star butcher (behind NYT's best burger in the world), blend takes burgers to a whole new level.

🍴 Go for... the Cheesy or the Signature. Their sweet potato fries are insane!

© Edouard Obeniche

🎯 Mon-Sun 12pm-11pm 📞 +33 1 42 49 28 35 💲 Casual Chic

@foodloversodyssey

URFA DÜRÜM
58, rue du Faubourg St Denis (10th)
Ⓜ Château d'Eau

The tiny shop doesn't look much, but these Kurdish sandwiches are the stuff of legend. People constantly line up here to taste some of their wrapped greatness. The stars of the menu are *lahmajouns*, thin and crispy Turkish pizzas filled with veggies and minced beef, straight out of the oven. The *dürüms* also deliver, with their skewers (lamb and/or chicken) and the house-baked flatbread. Everything is super-fresh here! No fat sauce added; the herbs and lime seasoning create all the magic.

🎯 Mon-Sat 12pm-12am / Sun 12pm-10pm

📞 +33 1 48 24 12 84 💲 Dive

L'AS DU FALAFEL
34, rue des Rosiers (4th) Ⓜ Saint-Paul

Ⓞ @lasdufalafel

Rue des Rosiers is this cute stretch in the heart of the old Jewish quarter. This green façade is an institution; so, there will anyway be a queue. Service is swift, though. The falafels are fantastic, and the pitas overflow with veggies (the roasted eggplant is a sweet addition). The room is cramped but, if you're fine with getting messy, the best way is to take away and munch it in the Marais alleyways.

🍴 Go for... the huge falafel special (light eaters can easily share one).

🎯 Mon-Thu 12pm-11pm / Fri 12pm-4pm
Sat 6:30pm-11pm / Sun 12pm-11pm

📞 +33 8 91 65 89 00 💲 Dive

GRUB ON THE GO -PRODUCER TO PLATE-

MARCHÉ DES ENFANTS ROUGES
39, rue de Bretagne (3rd) (M) Filles du Calvaire

If you're around le Marais, drop by this old-but-gold food market (the oldest in Paris). Hidden away behind big gates, this small courtyard is a local go-to place for world eats. Don't miss lunchtime! The market stays open in the p.m. but most stalls would close. Grab what tickles your fancy, and sit on the wooden benches. When the sun is filtering through, it's a pleasant plan.

🍳 Go for... the marvelous Moroccan food or the kickass blini-based sandwiches Chez Alain Miam Miam.

👑 Tue-Sat 8:30am-7:30pm $ Dive
    Sun 8:30am-2pm

MARCHÉ SAINT-QUENTIN
85 bis, boulevard Magenta (10th) (M) Gare de l'Est

Under the glass vaults of this beautiful covered market, you'll find food stalls with fresh produce and delis with all types of cuisine (Portuguese, African and what not). Tables and chairs are also set up such that, after feasting your eyes on cheeses and oysters, you can savour the food straightaway. The vibe is quintessentially Parisian and oh-so-charming. The soul of this diverse district is anchored right here.

🤤 Go for... the memorable chicken mafé at Oh Africa.

👑 Tue-Sat 8am-8pm / Sun 8am-1:30pm $ Dive
    Closed on Mon

GRUB ON THE GO -DELI'S DELIGHT-

© JP BALTEL

MAISON PLISSON
93, bd Beaumarchais (3rd) (M) St-Sébastien - Froissart

📷 @lamaisonplisson

The mission of this maison: source the best foodstuff and gather it all under one roof. In this beautiful place that's at once a bakery, a cellar, a high-end grocery store, a café, and a restaurant, you'll find quality staples and other varied niche products (gluten-free breads, regional finds, and more). If not on a Masterchef shopping hunt, sit for a coffee, a pastry, a meal made with fresh produce from the market, or take away some gourmet snacks from the deli.

👑 Tue-Sat 8:30am-9pm $ Casual Chic
    Sun-Mon 9:30am-8pm

LA GRANDE ÉPICERIE
38, rue de Sèvres (7th) (M) Sèvres - Babylone

📷 @lagrandeepicerie

The gourmet branch of Le Bon Marché (Paris oldest and iconic department store) is every foodie's dream come true. With its wide selection of goodies from the four corners of the world (and the finest French stuff), the place really has a wow factor. All you can think of is there: basics and rarities, chic and old school. Browsing the aisles is a delight in itself. But don't miss their deli section, which has lovely lunch treats.

👑 Mon-Sat 8:30am-9pm $ Casual Chic
    Sun 10am-8pm

PUR ETC.

 @puretc

Think good karma and good food go hand in hand? Step into this haven of feel-good fast food! Here, the veggies are seasonal and picked ripe, the meat is well fed and well treated, and all waste goes back to the earth through compost. Sourcing it all from small producers, these guys whip up fresh and simple all-homemade French cuisine. Plus, lunch just tastes so much better in their zero-waste reusable containers (those cute granny glass jars!) A fine lot of creative veg/vegan options are on the menu.

Go for... the Hachis Parmentier and the veg lasagne a la bolognaise.

25, rue Sedaine (11th) Ⓜ Bréguet Sabin
Mon-Fri 8:30am-10pm / Sat-Sun 10:30am-10pm

21, rue des Jeûneurs (2nd) Ⓜ Grands Boulevards
Mon-Fri 8:30am-5pm / Closed on weekends Dive

LIIFE

33, rue des Petits Carreaux (2nd) Ⓜ Sentier

 @liife_eatsmart

The Parisian pioneer of smart eating, this unique healthy joint caters to sporty folks (but not only them). Dishes are tailored to cater your workout: bodybuilding, detox, or cardio. Depending on your profile (fitness buff, weekend athlete, or healthy eater), pick amongst the veg, vegan, gluten-free, and hyper-protein options. The menu is filled with super aliments and fresh foodstuff.

Go for... the vegan Mac & Cheese. The Macorini, a veggie bake top for runners since lactose-free and filled with good carbs.

Mon-Fri 8:30am-5pm / Sat 10:30am-6pm
Closed on Sun
☎ +33 6 27 92 32 35 Dive

LES BOLS DE JEAN

2 rue Choiseul (2nd) Ⓜ Quatre-Septembre

📷 @bolsdejean

Here, we break the rules of savoir vivre and do away with plates! The wholesome cuisine concocted by Jean Imbert (Top Chef wonder boy) is served the old-school way, in bowls... made of bread. Created specially by star baker chef Eric Kayser, these edible casseroles hide delicate compositions: creative salads, restyled French classics, and gourmet dishes. All this comes with the finest artisan ingredients. The brioche-like texture of the bread will make you want to dip, nibble, and scrape your bowl off – an enjoyable experience.

Mon-Fri 11:30am-3:30pm / Thu-Fri 6:30pm-9:30pm
Sat 11:30am-9:30pm / Closed on Sun
☎ +33 1 44 76 00 58 Ⓢ Casual Chic

Not to mention... the veggie/vegan burgers, munchies and super desserts by **East Side Burgers**, a precious 100% veggie joint. - @estasideburgers

MODERN WESTERN

© Stéphane Adam

LE FLAMBOIRE

54, rue Blanche (9th) Ⓜ Blanche / Saint-Georges

🅞 @leflamboire

A *flamboir*, in old French, is a kitchen utensil that was used in the Middle Ages to baste the meat grilling in the rotisserie with melted lard. Dear veg friends, you got it: walk away! Basically, the tool looks like a mini funnel that you heat on the ember. Showered (with love and juices) and pampered, the cuts stay extra-tender and take on a superb smoky taste. The beef here comes from Aubrac, which produces the finest breed in France. So, needless to say, it's outstanding. The house-made chive sauce and the ratatouille are delish. If not in the mood for steak, there's also some fabulous fish on the menu. The large open wood-fire sits right in the dining room. So, you don't miss a morsel of the flame-grilled cooking.

 Go for... the côte de boeuf (beef rib). It's one kilo of roasted happiness.

🅺 Lunch: Tue-Sat 12pm-3pm
Dinner: Mon-Thu 6:30pm-11pm
Fri-Sat 6:30pm-11:30pm / Closed on Sun

🅒 +33 6 95 01 77 38   🆂 Fancy Pants

CANDELMA

73, rue de Seine (6th) Ⓜ Odéon

🅞 @candelmaparis

There is good old school pancakes... and there is Candelma, which is the pretty fine kind! With organic flour (gluten-free for the buckwheat) and top-notch fresh produce that's sustainably sourced, the pancakes earn their stripes and even dare to pull off a few eccentricities. The menu is a mix of restyled classics and original creations. Veg-friendly (tofu, truffle, veggies), most recipes come with a bit of a world food twist. The cider, too, is original: it's from the Basque country, not Brittany, and it's the bomb.

Go for... the Complète, a classic that never gets old... and only gets better here. The famous 'Mille Crêpes' is the highlight and a delight (a cake-like structure stuffed with praline and salted butter caramel). The "Et Bim" is basically a Tatin Tart in a pancake version.

🅺 Mon-Fri 12pm-2:30pm & 7pm-11pm
Sat 12pm-11pm / Sun 12pm-4pm

🅒 +33 9 52 29 78 79   🆂 Casual Chic

© Jérôme Galland

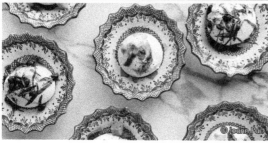
© Joann Pai

© Joann Pai

BIG MAMMA

* East Mamma - 133, rue du Faubourg Saint-Antoine (11th)
* Ober Mamma - 107, bld Richard Lenoir (11th)
* Mamma Primi - 71, rue des Dames (17th)
* Pizzeria Popolare - 111, rue Réaumur (2nd)
* Pink Mamma - 20bis, rue de Douai (9th)

📷 @bigmammagroup   💲 Casual Chic

Every evening, there are places in Paris that have customers lining up on the sidewalk. These are the Big Mamma venues. Some frowned and called it a fad, but time passed and Mamma has earned a name for herself. Her recipe is simple yet timeless: pasta and pizza that are authentic, tasty, wholesome, and come at mini prices. The secret, you ask? Ingredients brought from the motherland, 100% homemade, small producers, but big volumes. Bringing back the cheerful spirit of Italian trattorrias, Big Mamma guarantees happy vibes. The *squadra* is always warbling, laughing, whooping in Italian and acting pally. To keep things casual, it has a no-bookings rule. But if it's too busy when you show up, you can drop your name on the list, go for a drink, and come back.

There are six Mammas; yet, each has its own touch. First, there's **East Mamma,** the original trattoria, and **Mamma Primi,** the pasta paradise. Then, **Ober Mamma,** the aperitivo bar with its glass roof and big tree taking centre stage. That's where antipasti, Italian wines, and fab cocktails happen. **Pizzeria Popolare** has the soul of a Napolitan pizzeria, set in a stylish bar. Big communal tables blend into the dapper décor of the buzzing bar. The latest addition, **Pink Mamma,** sits at the heart of trendy SoPi and is the darling child – a stunning spot compiling the best of the rest. It occupies a whole (green-walled) building with incredible interiors, three levels, and a stellar rooftop.

🍽 Go for... the famous truffle pasta or the superb *stracciatella* (a creamy smoked burratta). Meat-wise, the pig bresaola and the *beef tagliata* (a matured cut, slow-roasted in the wood-fire oven) steal the show. At Pink Mamma, the go-to dish is called *bistecca alla fiorentina,* a big T-bone cooked in the Tuscan tradition. And if you drop by Pizzeria Popolare, make sure you try their buffalo milk gelatos, which are a treat.

MODERN WESTERN -NEO BISTROS-

VIVANT
43, rue des Petites Écuries (10th)
Ⓜ Cadet, Bonne Nouvelle
⊙ @vivantparis

This tiny and intimate place will make you feel special to be amongst the happy few the chef is cooking for. Behind his marble counter, prodigy Pierre whips up an honest ever-changing menu, following his whims and the seasonal market catches. The cellar overflows with natural gems. The homey candlelit space accommodates only a few tables; so, be sure to book! Else, head to Deviant - its sister venue next door, a drop-in tapas bar.

🍽 **Go for...** the pasta special or any fish dish (raw and cooked are both their forte).

✪ Mon-Fri from 7:30pm / Closed on weekends

☎ +33 1 42 46 43 55   Ⓢ Fancy Pants

@bozar_restaurant

LE RICHER
2, rue Richer (9th) Ⓜ Cadet, Bonne Nouvelle
⊙ @lericher_

This local joint has a no-booking rule, which makes it a pleasantly casual place. But the food will blow your random bistro expectations away. You'll get treated to beautifully presented plates, creative dishes, and a fresh menu reinvented every other week as inspiration and ingredients change. Resolutely modern yet honestly genuine, the setting and the cuisine (brightened up with a twist from the Japanese chef) are both on point.

✪ Mon-Sun 12pm-2:30pm & 7:30pm-10:30pm

☎ +33 9 67 29 18 43

Ⓢ Casual Chic

LE BARATIN
3, rue Jouye-Rouve (20th)
Ⓜ Pyrénées

This hole-in-the-wall bistro is as authentic as it gets. Here, the cuisine reflects the hosts: straightforward, zero fuss, but with lots of character. It's been thirty years that the chef has been consistently treating connoisseurs; yet, she never ceases to amaze. The set lunch is irresistible: twenty little euros, three courses and only a handful of daily specials on the blackboard (always a great hint). The organic wine list is exquisite. The promise of a memorable meal and a true Parisian experience. Among fine gourmets, it has even gained the reputation of being the best in town. Needless to say that early booking is a must.

✪ Tue-Fri 12pm-2:30pm & 7:30pm-11:15pm
Sat 7:30pm-11:15pm / Closed on Sun & Mon

☎ +33 1 43 49 39 70   Ⓢ Fancy Pants

MODERN WESTERN -SOUL FOOD-

MA BICHE
12, rue Véron (18th) Ⓜ Abbesses

Ma Biche is a modern take on granny cooking. Cause grans just know best; deal with it! The love behind honest-to-goodness old school cuisine and the creativity of a fresh generation of chefs. Bam! Meet Ma Biche, playfully restyling classics since 2014. Full farm-to-table vibe here, bringing a slice of the countryside to your plate. Teaming up with star farmers for top organic foodstuff and natural wines, they create earthy and hearty dishes. Drop by their homey nook in Montmartre for a memorable meal.

🍳 Go for... the homemade pork terrine and the killer burger.

🎴 Mon-Sun from 7pm
Brunch: Sat 12pm-2pm / Sun 12pm-3pm

📞 +33 1 42 58 22 20   💲 Casual Chic

LES AMIS DES MESSINA
81, rue Réaumur (2nd) Ⓜ Sentier
& 204, rue du Faubourg Saint Antoine (12th)
📷  @lesamisdesmessina

Need a fix of that warm Mediterranean vibe? Step into the superb rustic setting of this atrium that blends cellar, deli, market, kitchen, and dining room for a trip to Sicily. Sit at the wooden counter to share wine and antipasti, or under the skylight for something more substantial. Food here is a sensorial affair: you watch the enthralling ballet of the cooks and partake in the journey.

🍳 Go for... the antipasti.

Dozens of options and combinations: cured meats, cheeses ending in -a, tasty veggies and tutti quanti. Usually, that's enough to fill the stomach, but if not, their homemade gelatos are to die for (hazelnut, hands down!)

🎴 Mon-Sat 12pm-10:30pm   📞 +33 1 42 61 13 73   💲 Casual Chic
Closed on Sun

Not to mention... the impeccable Italian eats, enjoyed all day long in **Marcello's** lovely hidden sunken patio in the heart of Saint-Germain.
8, rue Mabillon (6th) @marcello._._._

MODERN WESTERN -CAVES À MANGER-

LA MANGERIE
7, rue de Jarente (4th) Ⓜ Saint-Paul

Ⓞ @lamangerie

The very idea of tapas is conviviality. This homey place is so warm that it feels like we've just landed at a friend's. It all starts with a welcome glass of rum put in your hands. After a chitchat with Charles, the owner (a darling! Yep, everyone is on first-name basis here), take a seat in the quirkily decorated room and relish one of their killer cocktails. It's always buzzing but in a fun way! Oh, also, don't get us wrong: we say « tapas » but it's rather fine fare in petite portions. Else, of course, there's always some jamon... Booking advised.

🍳 Go for... the mozzarella fritter and the Nutella tiramisu.

🕐 Mon-Sat 6pm-1am / Closed on Sun   Ⓒ +33 1 42 77 49 35   Ⓢ Casual Chic

SAUVAGE
60, rue du Cherche Midi (6th) Ⓜ Rennes

Ⓞ @cave_sauvage

This petite cave-cum-restaurant is a real find! Fine gourmets and wine buffs' fave, it's a bit of a gem, which will knock you off your feet. First, there's the impressive collection of natural wines that cover the walls: it's 120-reference long and filled with exciting finds. But it's also an outstanding fare in a ridiculously unassuming setting (read a hole-in-the-wall bistro with a miniature kitchen nestled at the back). The daily menu reads simple, through slashes (skipjack/pear/coriander) that perfectly sum up the humble and minimalistic approach. No big words or razzle-dazzle here — just fab produce, enhanced simply. A damn fine dining experience without frills. Count us in! But book to be sure, it's oh-so-tiny...

🕐 Tue-Sat 12:15am-2:15pm & 6:30pm-10:15pm   Ⓒ +33 6 88 88 48 23   Ⓢ Fancy Pants
Closed on Sun & Mon

MODERN WESTERN -CAVES A MANGER-

TERRA CORSA
42, rue des Martyrs (9th) (M) Pigalle
& Château d'Eau (10th)

Corsica, this Mediterranean gem of an island, boasts of some killer meat and cheese. This deli, packed with artisan Corsican goodies, has set up a tiny street-side terrace, where they serve the good stuff, along with a solid stock of wonderful wines. Enjoy their sweet set lunches (till 3pm) or come for aperitif. Plus, people-watching on the lovely Rue des Martyrs is a quintessential Parisian thing!

Go for... the mixed plate. You'll get to taste a bit of everything!

Mon-Sat 10:30am-9:30pm / Sun 10:30am-7pm

+33 1 48 78 20 70 $ Dive

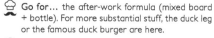

Ô COMPTOIR DU SUD-OUEST
167, rue Saint-Martin (3rd) (M) Rambuteau
& Miromesnil (8th)

@o_comptoir_du_sud_ouest

Oh joy! Oh bliss! Southwestern gastronomy has a home in Paris! Which means our share of fatty duck in all its forms, even the oh-so-infamous foie gras. Come indulge in this comforting (meat-heavy) cuisine in the place set up by local boy Thibault. This wine buff has handpicked every reference in his deli-cum-bistro; so, he is a savvy guide.

Go for... the after-work formula (mixed board + bottle). For more substantial stuff, the duck leg or the famous duck burger are here.

Tue-Sat 10am-12am / Sun 12pm-4pm
Mon 10am-4pm

+33 1 45 22 12 41 $ Casual Chic

GARE AU GORILLE
68, rue des Dames (17th) (M) Rome

@restaurantgareaugorille

Here, the tapas are reaching another level. The plates are small but the cuisine is grand. Packed with creativity and personality. The restaurant is one of the hottest in Paris and the chef is a young talent with a CV that makes heads spin. Yet, no fuss to be seen here – only a minimalist bistro décor and a casual ambiance. Dinner comprises beautiful plates (count three a head) or entire roasts to be shared, along with a selection of natural wines. Else, there is also the sweet three-course set lunch.

Mon-Fri 12:15pm-2pm & 7:30pm-10pm
Closed on weekends

+33 1 42 94 24 02 $ Fancy Pants

MODERN WESTERN -OLD SCHOOL-

© Thomas Pirel

BUFFET
8, Rue de la Main d'Or (11) (M) Ledru-Rollin

(O) @restaurantbuffet

This modern bistro sets out grandma porcelain and Moleskine leather seats; as French as it gets, right? But none of that retro trend-chasing here – the place and plates are genuinely old school. Unassumingly simple, the menu offers true French comfort food staples, mastered with panache. The natural wine picks just make it that much better, and the three-course set lunch, under 20 bucks, is an insane deal!

Go for... the timeless *blanquette de veau*.

Tue 7:30-11pm / Wed-Sat 12pm-2:30pm & 7:30pm-11pm
Closed on Sun & Mon

+33 1 83 89 63 82   ($) Dive

LE CAFÉ DE L'INDUSTRIE
16, rue Saint-Sabin (11th) (M) Bréguet Sabin

Cozy up in this café with a warm living room vibe. Everything here makes you want to linger: the subdued light, jazzy ambience and retro décor made of mismatched old paintings, palmtrees, vintage photos and exotic curios. The fare is the definition of comfort food: simple and soulful. This stalwart bistro is your best bet for honest-to-goodness in a hip neighbourhood. Just drop in and you'll feel instantly welcomed.

Mon-Sun 9am-2am

+33 1 47 00 13 53   ($) Casual Chic

CHEZ FERNAND
13, rue Guisarde (6th)
(M) Mabillon

(O) @chezfernandguisarde

Want hearty and traditional food as Granny would cook for the Sunday family lunch? Head to this Parisian institution! The super friendly staff will squeeze you into the main room that has a cheerful canteen vibe (they had communal tables before hipsters made it a thing).

Go for... the legendary beef Bourguignon. The baked Camembert is also a winner. If you're ready for snails, this is your go-to place. Oh, and their chocolate soufflé is killer!

Mon-Sun 12pm-2:30pm & 7pm-11pm
(12am on weekends)

+33 1 43 54 61 47   ($) Casual Chic

LA MARINE
55 bis, quai de Valmy (10th)
(M) République

Overlooking the canal Saint-Martin, La Marine is one pleasant lunch spot. Sit back on the heated terrace and watch life go by; or the quaint bistro inside has got some class too. Food is homemade, and the two-course set lunch is a sweet deal.
PS: Precious in Paris, they serve after French lunch times!

Go for... the great *gratin dauphinois*. On the sweet side, try their tasty Tatin tart.

Mon-Sun 7:30am-2am

+33 1 42 39 69 81   ($) Casual Chic

GIGI

4, rue de la Corderie (3rd) (M) Temple

@gigi_creperie

At Gigi's, you'll find way more than your classic jam pancake! Funky creations tickle your taste buds. First, there is the crêpe-apéro, restyled in the form of share bites. Then, the salads are also a surprise since they come in a bowl made out of a buckwheat galette. Everything is super-fresh and super-healthy: farm milk, eggs, and organic flour. The staff is adorable, the place charming and the lunch set a steal.

Go for... the Shiitaké, smoked ham, and Comté cheese galette.

Tue-Sat 12pm-10:30pm non-stop / Closed on Mon   +33 7 83 58 75 30   Dive

KRÜGEN

58, rue de la Fontaine au Roi (11th) (M) Goncourt, Parmentier

@krugen_paris

This deli, packed with goodies from Brittany, also serves authentic pancakes and buckwheat galettes in a stylish space. It's all made in-house, with the best foodstuff sourced from small producers on the Atlantic coast (*andouille*, artisanal sausage and jams). You can create your own galette with these marvelous meats, Camembert and top cheeses, veg confit... The ciders are super, of course. Also, there's Breizh beer.

Go for... the incomparable *complète*. The Kouign, a Breton sweet specialty pancake, is also worth a go. We've got a soft spot for the excellent chocolate and the divine salted-butter caramel.

Wed-Sat 12pm-2:30pm & 6:30pm-10:30pm   +33 9 52 29 78 79   Casual Chic
Sun 11:30am-4pm / Closed on Mon & Tue

MODERN WESTERN -MEAT FEAST-

CLOVER GRILL
6, rue Bailleul (1st) Ⓜ Louvre Rivoli

Ⓞ @clovergrillparis

Yes, simple steaks can be a byword for excellence. The evidence being, the grill joint created by Michelin-awarded star chef Jean-Francois Piège. The chic eatery gives top billing to exceptional meats (finest French and world-class dry-aged rarities), whose star cuts are displayed in a glass cabinet. Every bit is cooked to perfection in the rotisserie and served with dazzling side dishes.

© Nicolas Lobbestael

🍽 Go for... the *côte de bœuf*. Its rare breed, aged with beech tree, is phenomenal.

P.S: Early booking is a must. Else, lunch is more easy access (budget and schedule-wise).

❤ Mon-Sun 12pm-2:15pm & 7pm-10:30pm (11pm on weekends)   Ⓒ +33 1 40 41 59 59   Ⓢ Fancy Pants

BOUCHERIE ROULIÈRE
24, rue des Canettes (6th) Ⓜ Mabillon

Butchery has run in the Roulière family for five generations. Talk about tradition! The tiny meat shop from the start turned into an excellent bistro that celebrates simple classics. Taking particular care about meat quality, it offers gourmet carnivores (but not only!) some seriously solid meals. Roulière also masters the famous French food staples, such as foie gras or snails, as they are all artisanal.

🍽 Go for... the outstanding onion soup; it's truly the best in town! On the beef front, we're fans of the hand-cut tartare and the *entrecôte* (rib steak) with bone marrow.

❤ Mon-Sun 12pm-2:30pm & 7pm-11:30pm

Ⓒ +33 1 43 26 25 70   Ⓢ Casual Chic

BIEN ELEVÉ
47, rue Richer (9th) Ⓜ Grands Boulevards / Cadet

Ⓞ @restaurantbieneleve

This modern canteen serves sensational steaks, and yet retains a lovely unpretentious vibe. Their super sourcing truly hits the spot. The two young and friendly hosts indeed take excellent base products and serve them in simple yet elegant way. Meat is the main morsel here, but fish, sides (insane fries browned in meat fat!) and desserts are equally good. It's a local favourite (and a rather small spot); so, you better book.

🍽 Go for... the terrific tartare, topped with an *œuf parfait* yolk. Or the extra dry aged steak with a fab bearnaise.

❤ Tue-Sat 12pm-2pm & 7:30pm-10pm
Closed on Sun & Mon

Ⓒ +33 1 45 81 44 35   Ⓢ Casual Chic

 ⁵⁶ EAT

FICHON
98, rue Marcadet (18th) Ⓜ Marcadet Poissonniers

⊙ @fichon_boissonnier

Get on board this "cave à poisson", where fine fish meets stellar cellar. Cross-breeding with class, Fichon is a wine bar that changed tack by pairing organic wines with creative seafood. Drop by the Montmatre mother ship to taste their tapas, tartares, and tartines. Here, fish and shells are served in varied forms (even charcuterie!) Plates are pretty and tasty like those in fancy-schmancy eateries, but the vibe (and the bill) is way cooler. On the liquid front, some wonderful wines, artisanal brews, and cool cocktails.

🍳 **Go for...** the colourful ceviche or the trout confit.

✺ Tue-Sat 12:30pm-2:30pm & 7:30pm-10:30pm
Closed on Sun & Mon

☏ +33 9 70 94 52 14 $ Casual Chic

PLEINE MER
22, rue de Chabrol (10th) Ⓜ Poissonnière

This tiny, unassuming joint brings you bits of Brittany in Paris! The micro menu fits on one chalkboard: (organic) smoked salmon, (homemade) tarama, oysters and more oysters – just different sizes and types. Brought in straight from Cancale (the oyster hotspot on the Atlantic coast) daily, the shells are as fresh as it gets. In keeping with the authentic no-fuss vibe, it's served the purist way: with lemon, bread, and salted butter. The warm welcome from the producer-owner, the glass of white in the set lunch, and the delicious *kouign-amann* are just added bonus.

✺ Tue-Sat 10:30am-3pm & 4pm-10:30pm
Sun 10:30am-1pm / Closed on Mon

☏ +33 1 53 34 64 47 $ Casual Chic

BELLE MAISON
4, rue de Navarin (9th) Ⓜ Saint-Georges

⊙ @restaurant_belle_maison

The "Belle Maison" surely is one beautiful house. But its beauty does not lie only in its neat navy décor, ceramic walls, and designer raw wood fittings. The cuisine is the true showstopper. Inventive and delicate, it beautifully enhances the seafood without overdoing it. This fresh SoPi spot manages to ace the trendy and tasty in a winning formula.

👨‍🍳 **Go for...** the outstanding octopus. The whelks with their divine hay mayonnaise is a great way to get started, while their baba au rhum will ensure an epic ending.

✺ Tue-Sun 12:30am-2pm & 7:30pm-10pm (apéritif 6pm)
Closed on Sun & Mon

☏ +33 1 42 81 11 00 $ Fancy Pants

Not to mention... the lobster rolls and stellar snacks by **BULOT BULOT**, a cool seafood shack in Pigalle. @bulot_bulot_paris

MODERN WESTERN -CHEESY FIX-

LE CHALET SAVOYARD
58, rue de Charonne (11th) (M) Ledru-Rollin

Raclette, if you're just getting introduced to this heavenly specialty, is a cheese lover's dream come true. "Scraper" is the meaning in French, and yes, that's it: you will literally be scraping off cheese and eat it while it's still melting – an entire half wheel of it! An insane experience that you must try, if not lactose intolerant. This rustic-chic authentic eatery is your best bet for this in Paris. They also serve other cheese-based alpine stuff – fondue and tartiflette, which are just as delicious and generous. A word to the wise: come with an empty stomach! Booking advised.

Go for... the smoked cheese *raclette* or the cheese garlic and herbs fondue.

Mon-Sun 12pm-2:30pm & 7pm-11pm
Fri-Sat till 12am

+33 1 48 05 13 13

Casual Chic

@cderouvroy

HEUREUX COMME ALEXANDRE
24, rue de la Parcheminerie (5th)
(M) Cluny La Sorbonne / St-Michel
& Place Monge (5th)

(O) @heureuxcommealex

In a locale that's home to gazillions of seedy tourist traps, it's refreshing to find a joint like the one helmed by Alexandre! The quaint eatery is a cosy nook decorated with paintings, which also has a lovely terrace on the paved street. Fond of fondue? Two options: the cheesy (Savoyarde) or the meaty (Bourguignonne). In a communal pot, you dip bread into melted cheese or you boil meats. A fun and friendly meal to be shared – all the more pleasant in this personal place with Alexandre's attentive service.

Go for... the comforting cheese fondue.

Mon 6:30pm-11pm
Tue-Sun 12pm-2:30pm & 6:30pm-11pm

+33 1 43 26 49 66

Dive

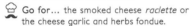

© Angela Pham

LE PETIT BLEU

23, rue Muller (18th) Ⓜ Château Rouge

This unassuming hole-in-the-wall eatery down the steps of Sacré-Coeur is a bit of a local best-kept secret. A steal of a deal, tasty eats, gigantic servings (seriously, a word to the wise: sharing is caring!), and the true taste of Tunisia... what else could one ask for? It's a no-fuss place, a little cramped and seedy, but folks visit mostly for the airy couscous and chilled beers.

Go for... the lamb tajine.

Mon 7pm-11:30pm / Tue-Sun 12pm-3pm & 7pm-11:30pm

+33 1 42 59 27 01 $ Dive

LE MÉCHOUI DU PRINCE

34-36, rue Monsieur le Prince (6th) Ⓜ Odéon

Ⓞ @mechouiduprince

This Latin Quarter landmark has the timelessness of places that never go out of style. The cosy oriental decor is restyled in a typical Parisian buidling (timber ceiling and exposed stone), which makes for a lovely setting. Authentic yet not over the top, it's your go-to place for outstanding Moroccan food.

Go for... the pastilla or the traditional Moroccan bricks to start, and a mint tea to wash it down!

Mon 7pm-11pm / Tue-Sun 12pm-3pm & 7pm-11pm

+33 1 85 15 21 42 $ Casual Chic

YEMMA

127, rue du Chemin Vert (11th) Ⓜ Père Lachaise / Rue St-Maur

Ⓞ @cantineyemma

Inspired by his mommy ("yemma"), Abdel Alaloui, the happy fellow mixing cooking and comedy on TV, set up this hip-cool Moroccan canteen. Teaming up with a food-trucker pal, he whips up street-style eats. Get in the game with some *kemia* (spreads and salads). Then, pick your bread (the *msemens*, those rich pancakes, are the bee's knees) and stuff it with meat and veggies. Else, there's the comforting couscous.

Go for... the lamb mechoui mesmen sandwich.

Mon-Sun 12pm-3pm & 7pm-11pm

+33 1 48 05 67 07 $ Dive

SALATIM

15, rue des Jeûneurs (2nd) Ⓜ Sentier

Ⓞ @salatim_paris

Colourful plates and killer sandwiches are on the menu of this kosher canteen. It's a cheerful neighbourhood joint, with its regulars, daily specials and staples playing cards. Just like in Tel-Aviv, sip a green glass of *limonada* (frozen mint lemonade) to stay fresh.

Go for... the heavenly hummus, excellent eggplant dip and brilliant babka Heads-up: Wednesday is Schnitzelday and it's sensational.

Tue-Thu 8:30am-11pm / Fri-Mon 8:30am-4pm
Sun 10am-4pm / Closed on Sat

+33 1 42 36 30 03 $ Dive

FAR-FLUNG FLAVOURS

@chopchicksinparis

© Thomas Smith

HERO

289, rue St Denis (2nd) Ⓜ Strasbourg - Saint-Denis

🅞 @hero_paris

This cool Korean joint is definitely a local hero! Its cocktails are at the top of their game, and its fusion food is fab. It looks classy – all dimly lit and neatly put together – but it's refreshingly low-key and cheap. Their set lunch is an awesome deal! Share a few plates and enjoy the 90's hip-hop playlist. Hero is quite a hit; so, booking is a safe bet.

🍴 Go for... the fried chicken; it's the rockstar! Cooked on point, juicy and divinely crispy, it's finger-lickingly good. Indecise? The platter brings you the three types (garlic, chili, and classic) in one. The pork buns are also phenomenal. On the veg side, the kimchi is great. To drink, the Makolada is a must!

🅒 Tue-Sun 12am-2:30pm & 7pm-11pm / Closed on Mon   📞 +33 1 42 33 38 01   Ⓢ Casual Chic

@barbugourmand

STREET BANGKOK

3, rue Eugène Varlin (10th) Ⓜ Château-Landon
& 13, rue de la Roquette (11th)

Exotic eats as tasty as in Thai streets, but in a cooler setting! Dishes here are superbly seasoned (spicy enough for the sharp palates) and simmered for hours by expert chefs from Bangkok. The neon-lit décor immerses you in a vibrant urban vibe. On the menu, three set meals to compose from fresh salads, tangy craft drinks, skewers smothered in sauce, over jasmine rice. Grab a bamboo tray and sip on a signature "draft" – read, one of their kooky Asian-inspired cocktails. The friendly BKK team will only add to this sweet time!

🍴 Go for... the lamb curry and the beef salad (well, make it all three salads! The pork and papaya are also worth a go).

🅒 Mon-Sun 12pm-11pm   📞 +33 1 42 05 22 51   Ⓢ Dive

NANASHI
57, rue Charlot (3rd) Ⓜ Filles du Calvaire
& 31, rue de Paradis (10th)

📷 @nanashi_paris

Organic hip meets authentic Japanese – that's roughly how we can sum up this healthy canteen. Adding her unique modern spin and a touch of fusion, the chef created the "Parisian bento" (a lunchbox that comes in a veg, fish, or meat version). She makes it a point to buy local and organic, and to make everything in-house. Add restyled Japanese staples, fresh juices, plus yummy desserts, and any healthy foodie will have a soft spot for Nanashi. Their minimal yet delicate cooking is a delight.

👨‍🍳 Go for... the bento du jour and the chocolate-yuzu fondant cake.

👨‍🍳 Mon-Wed 12pm-3pm & 8pm-11pm
Thu-Sun 12pm-3pm & 7:30pm-11pm

📞 +33 9 60 00 25 59   💲 Dive

HAKATA CHOTEN
53, rue des Petits Champs (1st) Ⓜ Pyramides

Squeeze into this busy joint and get a fix of authentic Japanese eats. On the menu, *gyozas* (dumplings) and *tonkatsu ramen* (noodle and pork soups). The steaming bowls of tasty broth are comforting to bits, but the juicy and crispy gyozas steal the show. It's a little drop-in only spot. So, be prepared to wait a bit. Come early!

👨‍🍳 Go for... the pork or leek gyozas, the miso chashu (braised pork) ramen.

👨‍🍳 Mon-Sat 12pm-3pm & 7pm-10pm

📞 +33 1 40 20 98 88   💲 Dive

LE PETIT CAMBODGE
20, rue Alibert (10th) Ⓜ Goncourt
& 4, rue Beaurepaire (10th)

📷 @lepetitcambodge

Feeling like a fresh and light lunch? Bobun it is, then! Get a little breath of exotic air with their tasty Cambodian-style fare, filled with peanut, coriander, and other exotic flavours. This low-key spot along the Canal Saint-Martin is the hangout for a young and cool crowd. It's always buzzing, tables are shared, and so are nems and conversation, in an upbeat hubbub that's part of the charm.

👨‍🍳 Go for... the shrimp bobun. If you need some comforting warmth, there's the Natin and its fish-meet-meat savour. And to spice things up, you have the chicken curry.

👨‍🍳 Mon-Sun 12pm-11pm non stop (11:30pm Sat-Sun)

📞 +33 1 42 45 80 88   💲 Dive

LA VILLA PAPILLON
15, rue Tiquetonne (2nd) Ⓜ Etienne Marcel

📷 @villapapillonofficielle

For terrific Thai eats, head to this joint helmed by the fantastic Tik. Regulars keep coming back for the soulful and flavourful food she concocts. It's fresh and as authentic as it gets (the Thai folks' go-to for a taste of home). The buzzing friendly vibe is infectious. Booking advised.

👨‍🍳 Go for... the duck confit samosas, chicken taro nems, or shrimp dumplings in coconut sauce. Lots of veg options on the menu as well.

👨‍🍳 Mon-Fri 12pm-3pm & 7pm-9pm / Sat-Sun 7pm-9pm

📞 +33 1 42 21 44 83   💲 Casual Chic

BREAKY, COFFEE & MORE

@luciatalkspictures

@amauryzep

SEASON

1, rue Charles Francois Dupuis (3rd) Ⓜ République
& Season Market: 98, rue de Turenne (3rd)

📷 @seasonparis

Gomasio, kale, acai, quinoa, spelt... if these aren't foreign and sound sweet to your ears, you may have found your canteen in Season. The menu of this hip eatery, with a bit of an L.A. vibe, is indeed decidely healthy. The hungry type? No stress! Season is not just about seeds and fruits! They also offer some seriously hearty stuff with a healthy twist, such as the burger made with gluten-free bread. It's a popular spot, often busy and drop-in only, which means a bit of a wait and not much lingering.

 Go for... the wholesome bowls, with their rainbow of colours. The granola comes in a variety of combos, mixing fresh and dried fruits, nuts and seeds. Pancakes are also a beautiful treat.

🅚 Mon-Sat 8:30am-1am
Sun 8:30am-7pm (food till 4pm)

🅒 +33 9 67 17 52 97

BOOT CAFÉ

19, rue du Pont aux Choux (3rd) Ⓜ St-Sébastien - Froissart
& 26, rue des Grands Augustins (6th) Ⓜ Odéon

📷 @bootcafe

"This coffee is made for walking." This handwritten quote on the window refers to...

a/ the fact that the café is housed in an old cobbler shop;
b/ the super limited seating in the pocket-sized and, therefore, grab-and-go spot.

A bit of both since Boot is literally the teeniest-tiniest coffeeshop in Paris (maybe even the world) but certainly also one of the cutest. Its quaint blue storefront in le Marais is one of the most Instagramed in town. But it's more than just a pretty face; the coffee specially is wow! A second Boot Café (a wee larger and cosier) appeared in St-Michel, and it's just as charming. The menu, too, is more extensive, with a few salad and world-food-inspired additions.

 Go for... their yummy chocolate chip oatmeal cookies. The delicious cappuccino or the flavoursome cortado will leave you all set to re-boot.

🅚 Mon-Sun 10am-6pm

🅒 +33 1 73 70 14 57   🅒 +33 6 26 41 10 66

@morganabbou

MOKONUTS

5, rue Saint-Bernard (11th) (M) Faidherbe - Chaligny

(O) @mokonutsbakery

"Made with love" is not just a way of speaking here. Soul, love, and care are infused in every plate prepared by Moko and Omar, the lovely couple behind the artisanal and personal Mokonuts. The café-bakery is their labour of love. The place is small only to keep things intimate and honest; and if they are not more open, it's to keep time for their girls, as this is just a two-person team. She is Japanese and she bakes. He is Lebanese and he cooks. Together, they offer a creative healthy-but-tasty menu that changes daily. It is organic with a Mediterannean touch.

Go for... the out-of-this-world multigrain chocolate cookies. Freshly baked many times a day, they stay soft and chewy.

PS: Try to give them a call if you're dropping in for lunch since the place is very tiny and a local love.

Mon-Fri 8:45am-6pm / Closed on weekends

+33 9 80 81 82 85

BREAKY, COFFEE & MORE -COFFEE CHAMPS-

RADIO DAYS
15, rue Alibert (10th) Ⓜ Goncourt

🅞 @radiodays.cafe

In this inviting blue joint, the first to catch attention is R2D2. Taking centre stage, the customised vintage-style espresso machine sets the tone. Along with the killer specialty coffee, you can dig into Manu and Beebo's collection of vinyles and comics or just cosy up to the sound of their cool playlist and chat with these two darlings. Add to this the comforting soups and pastries, and the place is damn homey!

🍽 **Go for...** the delicious homemade granola and the fantastic filter coffee.

🎯 Mon, Wed, Thu & Fri 8:30am-5pm
Sat-Sun 10am-6pm / Closed on Tue

@luciatalkspictures

@luciatalkspictures

LOMI
3 ter, rue Marcadet (18th) Ⓜ Marcadet Poissoniers

🅞 @cafelomi

These four little letters make up a big name in the Paris specialty coffee scene. Read between the lines of sourcing lists and you'll find their beans in many of the top joints in town. Originally a roastery and a training academy, this team of enthusiasts also opened an on-site café to keep sharing the love.

🍽 **Go for...** the impeccable lattes. If you're the adventurous type, they have something called "café fromage" that's pretty rad. Cheese-meet-coffee: only in Paris, right? A one-of-a-kind.

🎯 Mon-Fri 8am-6pm / Sat-Sun 10am-7pm

☎ +33 9 80 39 56 24

TEN BELLES
10, rue de la Grange aux Belles (10th) Ⓜ Jacques Bonsergent
& Ten Belles Bread: 17-19, rue Bréguet (11th)

🅞 @tenbelles

The pioneer of Parisian coffee shops hasn't lost any of its mojo. It's only getting better and bigger: they just opened a sister venue that delivers beautiful baked goods. But we've got a soft spot for the original location, off the Canal Saint-Martin. It's a tiny refuge that serves beautiful coffee. It's also a real bakery, and their organic artisan bread is otherworldly.

🎯 Mon-Fri 8am-5pm / Sat-Sun 9am-6pm

☎ +33 1 42 40 90 78

© Ten Belles

Not to mention... the top-notch coffee and croissants at **KOZY**. Your best bet to avoid tourist traps when sightseeing near the Champs Elysées or the Eiffel Tower! - @kozyparis

BREAKY, COFFEE & MORE -QUIRKY REFUGES-

THE HOOD
80, rue Jean-Pierre Timbaud (11th) Ⓜ Parmentier
📷 @thehoodparis

Behind the vintage façade of this 70's grocery store sits a coffee shop with a soul that will steal your heart. Hangout of the cool freelancers (it's also a co-working space) and musicos (they host jam sessions and acoustic gigs), it's a laid-back place with a warm sense of community. It is just the kind of place you feel like cosying up in, whiling away the hours and connecting with the local crowd. For fuel, they serve up specialty coffee, yummy homemade pastries, and healthy Asian-inspired eats. The menu gets refreshed daily; so, you can make it your hood! It's multicultural, with a bit of a Brooklyn vibe, so obviously super English-friendly!

🍽 Go for... the Asian-style iced coffee and the carrot cake.

🕐 Mon, Wed, Thu & Fri 9.30am-5.30pm / Sat-Sun 10am-6pm / Closed on Tue　　📞 +33 1 43 57 20 50

LA RECYCLERIE
83, boulevard Ornano (18th) Ⓜ Porte de Clignancourt
📷 @larecyclerie

For a more offbeat breed of fun, venture off the city centre and swing by the edgy northern fringe of Paris. There awaits a funky nature retreat. Sitting in an abandoned train station, this unique spot is a greenie paradise. At once an urban farm, a community garden, a repair workshop, an organic canteen, a market, a collaborative space based on ethical values, a library, and a bag of other cool stuff to discover. An entire playground to explore, with nooks and crannies – both inside and outside, along the tracks. It's a lovely daytime spot to chill! The vibe is relaxed, a little hipster-ish of course, but not overdoing it. An inspiring place.

🕐 Mon-Sun 8am-10pm　　　　　　　📞 +33 01 42 57 58 49

EAT 65

BREAKY, COFFEE & MORE -FRENCH TOUCH-

CAFÉ MARLETTE
rue des Martyrs (9th) Ⓜ Pigalle / Saint-Georges
& 63, rue du Faubourg Poissonnière (9th)

Ⓞ @marlettecake

Marlette is the fairy that makes organic baking easy-peasy. Offering a wide range of mixes to whip up wholesome cakes at home, the brand has also set up cafés where you get treated to their tasty pastries (all made in-house with their mixes). The beautiful brunch options are made with fantastic produce sourced from Parisian artisans, most of them located in the very same Rue des Martyrs, which is a true gourmet heaven. Heads-up, set breakfasts are super hearty, so sharing is in order.

🥢 Mon-Fri 8:30am-7pm / Sat-Sun 9:30am-7pm

📞 +33 1 43 55 60 10

UPTOWN
18, rue Francoeur (18th) Ⓜ Lamarck Caulaicourt

Ⓞ @uptown.paris

You'll have to climb uptown to get to this blue-painted chalet, but it's worth the effort, as the brunch here does really stand out! Of a rather delicate calibre, the menu restyles classics with flair and a gastronomic twist. Taking the finest foodstuff and enhancing it in a subtle, inventive way, the menu is top-notch – not to mention the killer cocktails and imported wines. To balance all this awesomeness, the decor keeps it simple and authentic (untreated wood and bricks). No hype, no fuss, just the essential. The sweet addition is their terrace (heated in winter).

🥢 Mon 7pm-1am / Tue-Fri 5pm-1am / Sat-Sun 11:30am-1am

📞 +33 1 84 05 62 79   💲 Fancy Pants

CAFÉ OBERKAMPF
3, rue Neuve Popincourt (11th) Ⓜ Parmentier

Ⓞ @cafeoberkampf

In the small room or behind the counter, you can hear French and English wafting around, mixing with the exquisite smell of coffee. With its terrific tartines and cool vibe, this hole-in-the-wall café, helmed by a Brit, has quickly become the hangout of a cosmopolitan crowd. A mini coffee shop (only a tiny dozen of seats) but with maxi appeal.

👨‍🍳 Go for... the banana bread, served grilled with salted butter melting. The dirty chai (a chai latte doubled with a shot of espresso) is a phenomenal creation.

🥢 Mon, Tue & Fri 8:30am-4:30pm / Sat-Sun 9:30am-4:30pm
Closed on Wed & Thu

📞 +33 1 43 55 60 10

BREAKY, COFFEE & MORE -EN VOGUE-

HÔTEL AMOUR

8, rue Navarin (9th) Ⓜ Pigalle / Saint-Georges
& Hotel Grand Amour: 18, rue de la Fidelité (9th)

◎ @hotelamour

With a name that oozes romance, a decadent décor, an artsy-chic vibe, and a hidden garden, this hotel is the go-to destination for lovers, but mostly for the hip SoPi bunch. Open all-day, it's a cosy refuge and a glamorous hotspot for daytime breaks, late-night snacks and whatnot. The food is fairly traditional, mixing French and American classics, but always on point. A few brunch specials add to the regular menu on weekends.

🍽 **Go for...** the divine chocolate madeleines, freshly baked for brunch. There's also the comforting mac and cheese in their French version (Comté cheese and ham).
P.S. Its sister venue, the Grand Amour, Rue de la Fidelité (oui, oui...), with its pretty patio, is charming as well.

✹ Mon-Sun 8am-2am   ☎ +33 1 48 78 31 80

© François Coquerel

@luciatakspictures

THE BROKEN ARM

12, rue Perrée (3rd) Ⓜ Temple

◎ @thebrokenarm

It is first and foremost a niche concept store, lair of the edgy fashionistas. The kind of minimalist sleek space, with a handful of carefully selected items, unique finds and cool design books. But don't feel intimidated if you're not from the fashion sphere! The vibe is very chilled, and the bright adjacent café super cosy! In a Scandinavian decor, they serve a daily salad, soup and sandwich, all fresh and made in-house. The chef is brilliant, and the coffee is top-notch.

✹ Tue-Sat 9am-6pm   ☎ +33 1 44 61 53 60
   Closed on Sun & Mon

CAFÉ KITSUNÉ

51, galerie de Montpensier (1st)
Ⓜ Palais Royal Musée du Louvre

◎ @cafekitsune

Kitsuné, hip French fashion-meet-electro label (see p.76), also has its coffee shop. Like its Tokyo twin, it's the hangout of a fashion-forward globetrotting crowd. In keeping with their Franco-Japanese touch, the menu gets a matcha takeover. The coffee is fabulous, the sweets gluten-free and the cold-pressed juices hyper-healthy. It's a hole-in-the-colonnade spot (inside the Palais Royal), so it's a must to take away and sit in the lovely gardens.

✹ Mon-Sun 10am-6:30pm   ☎ +33 1 40 15 62 31

BREAKY, COFFEE & MORE -FEEL-GOOD FOOD-

JAH JAH BY LE TRICYCLE
11 rue des Petites Écuries (10th) Ⓜ Château d'Eau

Ⓘ @letricycle

It all started with meals on wheels, but no food truck here: it was the greenie version. Le Tricycle was the first food bike in Paris. The wandering duo then settled down and Jah Jah was born. It is a truly unique joint to say the least, since vegan here gets funked-up in rasta version. Like any other healthy eatery, the menu is made of bowls, soups, and cold-press juices but, unlike anywhere else, it also features a restyled veg hot dog and inventive snacks in the same vein. It's so tasty that it even wins over the vegan-sceptics.

🕗 Wed-Mon 12pm-3pm & 7pm-10pm / Brunch on Sun
Closed on Tue

☏ +33 1 46 27 38 03

LE BICHAT
11, rue Bichat (10th) Ⓜ Goncourt / République

Ⓘ @lebichat

This is the dream canteen. Not only does it offer fresh and wholesome homemade meals at decent prices, but it's also what soul food is all about. Infused with ethical values of slow food, the fare is seasonal, organic, simple and as local as possible, to make the quality accessible to most and fair to all. The initiative of a social activist, Le Bichat promotes a positive food waste attitude (the old school way, using glass jars). Every day, one soup, three cakes, and one bowl – a rice-veggie base plus one extra (eggs, fish, chicken, or veg) are offered. In keeping with their philosophy, it's a collaborative place, so don't be surprised by the self-service!

🕗 Mon-Sun 9am-11pm

☏ +33 9 54 27 68 97

Ⓢ Dive

CAFÉ PINSON
6, rue du Forez (3rd) Ⓜ Filles du Calvaire
& 58, rue du Faubourg Poissonnière (10th)

Ⓘ @cafepinson

Since healthy can also be funky, meet Pinson! It is a refuge of well-being and well-eating which, on top of being organic, is also chic. What great fun is this cosy, pretty joint and its neat interior design! It just brightens the sometimes a-tad-too-pure routine of vegan foodies. Killing two birds with one stone, this is a Scandinavian-style blue boudoir with a vegetarian (vegan as much as one can) fare packed with superfoods. The menu sticks to the essential (four entries, three mains, and a handful of desserts), and changes often to stay the freshest.

© Philippe Lévy

🍽 Go for... the "madeleines de l'impossible" (wheat- and butter-free)

🕗 Mon-Fri 9am-10pm / Sat 10am-10pm
Sun 12pm-6pm (brunch at 12pm and 2:30pm)

☏ +33 9 83 82 53 53

BREAKY, COFFEE & MORE -FULL BREAKFAST-

© Nico Alary © Nico Alary

HOLLYBELLY 5

5, rue Lucien Sampaix (10th) Ⓜ Jacques Bonsergent

📷 @holybellycafe

Need a break from espresso and croissants? Hollybelly has brought hash brown, bacon, and Melbourne-style flat-whites to town! On communal tables, in a laidback and friendly vibe quite typical of Aussie hospitality, get a simple but spot-on breaky with a creative twist. The coffee meets Australian standards, read excellent.

Go for... the house granola and the (sweet or savoury) stack of pancakes. The homemade sausage patties and hash brown are impeccable. Crisp bacon and velvety eggs are mastered classics that don't disappoint. On the veg side, the black rice porridge wins.

Mon-Sun 9am-5pm   📞 +33 1 82 28 00 80

© Natalie Tusznio

HARDWARE SOCIÉTÉ

Montmartre (18th) Ⓜ Lamarck Caulaincourt

📷 @hardwaresocieteparis

At the feet of the Sacré Coeur sits this not-so-secret of a gem. If all the climbing and exploring gets you hungry, stop at this cute cafe for a killer Aussie-inspired brunch. These folks from Melbourne, the crowned breakfast capital of the world (where they created the Hardware mothership), exported the Melbourne formula and put their unique spin on French classics. Their artisanal coffee is top-notch, especially the lattes. The food is fresh, creative, and beautifully presented! Just be prepared for a little wait on the weekend brunch.

Go for... the pain perdu brioche; it's to die for!

Mon, Thu & Fri 9am-4pm / Sat-Sun 9:30am-4:30pm
Closed on Tue & Wed

📞 +33 1 42 51 69 03

ECHO

95, rue d'Aboukir (2nd) Ⓜ Sentier

📷 @echo_deli

Want to spice up your brunch, lunch, and everything in between? This colourful Californian canteen is the season's hottest sensation, bringing sunshine directly to your plate. A chef freshly landed from L.A., with a few hits under her belt, has made grilled cheese great again. Halfaway where gourmet meets gluten-free, Echo whips up a comfort food that raises the bar. Local ingredients for XXL sandwiches and fresh creations; yes, please!

Go for... the brilliant bacon veggie (shiitakes with chipotle and maple syrup), the marvellous masala chai cookie, and the divine rose-cucumber soda. The Mexican chorizo sandwich is a star!

Wed-Fri 9am-4pm   📞 +33 1 40 26 53 21
Sat-Sun 10am-5pm
Closed on Mon & Tue

EAT ⁶⁹

Sweet Treats

The top dessert delights to enjoy in Paris

a marvelous mont blanc cake at the Belle Époque tea salon Angelina.
To pair with their divine hot chocolate

a terrific Tatin Tart by Karamel, or another of their caramel-loaded goodies

a memorable macaron by master chef Pierre Hermé
One-of-a-kind delicate flavours and a ganache to die for!

a phenomenal Paris-Brest by chocolate whiz Jacques Genin, or another of his made-to-order killer creations.

a legendary artisan ice-cream
by Berthillon

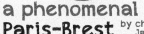

a creative gourmet éclair
by L'Éclair de Génie

Angelina 226, rue de Rivoli (1er) Ⓜ Concorde / Tuileries	◎ @angelina_paris	Mon-Sun 7:30am-7pm	+33 1 42 60 82 00
Jacques Genin 113, rue de Turenne (3e) Ⓜ République	◎ @jacquesgenin	Tue-Sun 11am-7pm Closed on Mon	+33 1 45 77 29 01
Berthillon 29-31, rue Saint-Louis en l'Île (4e) Ⓜ Pont Marie	◎ @berthillon_officiel	Wed-Sun 10am-8pm Closed on Mon & Tue	+33 1 43 54 31 61
Karamel 67, rue Saint-Dominique (7th) Ⓜ Invalides	◎ @karamel_paris_officiel	Mon-Sun 8:30am-8pm	+33 1 71 93 02 94
Pierre Hermé 72, rue Bonaparte (6e) Ⓜ Saint-Sulpice & Marais, Concorde, Galeries Lafayette	◎ @pierrehermeofficial	Mon-Sun 10am-7pm	+33 1 43 54 47 77
L'Éclair de Génie 32, rue Notre Dame des Victoires (2e) Ⓜ Bourse & Odéon, Marais, Montmartre, Montorgueil, BHV, Galeries Lafayette	◎ @leclairdegenieofficiel	Mon-Sat 10am-7pm Closed on Sun	+33 1 40 15 61 07

LE DALI (MEURICE HOTEL)

228, rue de Rivoli (1st) Ⓜ Concorde / Tuileries

📷 @cedricgrolet, @lemeuriceparis

Saying Cédric Grolet, the pastry chef of this palace-hotel, is "the best" is no understatement since he got crowned the official world title. What he does is truly spectacular, utterly beautiful, and simply fun. He creates magic by crafting surreal true-to-life fruit pastries. His pieces are so wow that they have become huge Instagram hits. Needless to say, tea time here takes things to another level! The indulgence includes a selection of baked goods (somptuous scones, among others) and savoury snacks, but you can add the funkier creations *à la carte* (on weekdays only). What's sweet, the service is attentive but not even a little stiff! An exceptional experience over all.

P.S. Book a few weeks ahead, considering chef Grolet's popularity.

💡 **Extra Tip:** If you can't make it to the Meurice, note that Cédric Grolet just opened a pastry shop in the 1rst arrondissement (6, rue de Castiglione, a stone's throw away from the Place Vendôme palace).

🐱 Mon-Sun 3:30pm-6pm

📞 +33 1 44 58 1010

®pmonetta

®pmonetta

CARETTE

25, place des Vosges (3rd) Ⓜ Saint-Paul, Bastille
& 4, place du Trocadéro (16th)

📷 @caretteofficiel

This teahouse, that's been around since the 20's, is one of those places that have endured through decades while retaining a cute old-world charm. With its prime locations in town (on the Trocadéro, overlooking the Eiffel Tower, and on the lovely Place des Vosges), Carette is an institution famed for its chocolat chaud and artisanal pastries. The hot chocolate is sublime (thick and rich) and comes with its own silver serving set. The whipped cream is out of this world.

🍽 **Go for...** the chocolate. Enough said. For a solid bite, the Mille-feuille is delightful.

🐱 Mon-Sun 7am-11:30pm   📞 +33 1 48 87 94 07

Bakers Masters

Paris is home to a gazillion of awesome bakeries but we managed to shortlist a few faves. Special shout-out to...

MAISON LANDEMAINE
41, rue Oberkampf (11th) Ⓜ Oberkampf & one in every arrondissement

⊙ @maisonlandemaine

for their dozen organic specialty breads (fruity, nutty, gluten-free...), all artisanal and traditional

🍞 **Go for...** the impeccable pain au chocolat, one of the best you'll find in Paris. The pink praline brioche is a regional specialty that's well worth a go!

✖ Closed on Wed

MAMICHE
45, rue Condorcet (9th) Ⓜ Anvers

⊙ @boulangeriemamiche

for the creative twist brought in by the two young girls at the helm of this bubbly bakery

MAMICHE

🍞 **Go for...** the Babka, an insane chocolatey brioche, the airy chouquettes or their divinely puffy pain au chocolat

✖ Closed on Sun

BLÉ SUCRÉ
7, rue Antoine Vollon (12th) Ⓜ Ledru-Rollin

⊙ @ble_sucre

for their madeleines — the best in town, and their beautiful viennoiseries, credits to the ex- palace pastry chef who opened his unassuming neighborhood den

la madeleine du partage

🍞 **Go for...** the caramelized kouign-amann; it's the star of the pastry section!

✖ Closed on Mon

GÉRARD MULOT
76, rue de Seine (6th) Ⓜ Mabillon / Odéon

⊙ @maisonmulot

for their marvelous macarons, delicate pastries, fab fruit tarts and quiches

🍞 **Go for...** their signature Amaryllis, that mixes tangy raspberries, creamy vanilla and an almond macaron

✖ Closed on Wed

MAISON KAYSER
18, rue du Bac (7th) Ⓜ Rue du Bac & Louvre, Odéon, Monge, Réaumur...

⊙ @maisonkayser

for their yummy cheese bread, specialty loaves and viennoiseries

ERIC KAYSER

🍞 **Go for...** the delicious cookies

✖ Closed on Mon

PAIN PAIN
88, rue des Martyrs (18th) Ⓜ Pigalle / Abbesses

⊙ @painpain_paris

for their beautiful baguette, which got crowned the Parisian title, but also for their gorgeous gougere breads and tasty cakes

🍞 **Go for...** the mandel croissant and the chocolate/pistachio brioche bun

✖ Closed on Mon

SHOP

MARKETS

© Marc Bertrand / Paris Tourist Office

PUCES DE SAINT-OUEN
Ⓜ Garibaldi

Among the largest flea markets in the world, « Les Puces » is a standalone destination even if you're not on vintage shopping mode. Let's say, it looks like a big, open-air museum where Art Deco antiques jostle for space with gold mirrors, chandeliers and Napoleon III cabinets. Even if the stuff is not your style or within budget, it's fun just to browse! The stroll is enchanting, timeless. And yes, you can find some affordable treasures (vintage toys, glassware...). It's a maze, though, and you'll need a roadmap: Rue des Rosiers is the main street, and off this stretch meander a series of markets:

Marché Vernaison keeps faith with the original spirit of the flea market. It's diverse, full of surprises, the narrow, picturesque alleys hiding quirky finds. The covered **Marché Dauphine** is where to go for artsy buys: crumbling books, yellowed photos, vinyl records, cinema posters and music gear. The open-air **Marché Paul Bert - Serpette** is higher-end (home to 19th-20th century furniture), but it's a great place to window shop in.

You can easily spend the whole day here, so for fuel head to **Flea**, a lovely coffee-shop-cum-cabinet-of-curiosities.

🔆 **Extra tip:** Visit in the morning, or even better, on a Monday.

🗓 Sat-Sun 10am-6pm / Mon 11am-5pm / Closed Tue-Fri

© Thierry Daniel - Paris Tourist Office

MARCHÉ AUX FLEURS
Allée Célestin Hennion (4th) Ⓜ Cité

Notre Dame, of course. But the Cité Island is home to much more. A picturesque flower market is housed in beautiful metal pavilions from the 1900's. It's a cute place for a stroll, even if you are no flower fanatic. On Sundays, the place fills with the tweet of birds and you can meet exotic species here. If you are visiting, take a bucolic tour, drown in birdsong

🗓 Flowers: Mon-Sun 8am-7:30pm
Birds: Sun 8am-7pm

© Gavroche Père & Fils

MARCHÉ D'ALIGRE
Place d'Aligre (12th) Ⓜ Ledru-Rollin

Want to experience a typical market, *à la parisienne?* This is it. It's vibrant, cheerful, no-nonsense and easy on the wallet. Vendors are hailing patrons and joking around; local folk are catching up at the café. The market splits into three parts: the covered market (Marché Beauveau), the flea market for good bargains, and the Rue d'Aligre, a line-up of fresh food stalls.

🍽 Go for... the phenomenal pastries at Jojo&Co, La Pâtisserie du Marché. The cheese shop at the entrance to the covered market is the bee's knees!

🕙 Tue-Fri 9am-1pm & 4pm-7:30pm / Sat 9am-1pm & 3:30pm-7:30pm
Sun 9am-1:30pm / Closed on Mon

MARCHÉ BASTILLE
8, boulevard Richard Lenoir (11th) Ⓜ Ledru-Rollin

One of the biggest in town, this local market is always bustling and packed with foodie goodies. With the Bastille column as backdrop and the Canal Saint-Martin under your feet, immerse yourself in one of the most atmospheric Parisian neighbourhood. The street musicians only add to the friendly vibes.

🍽 Go for... the freshly made crêpes. There's also a stall where you can taste oysters on the spot, along with a glass of white.

🕙 Thu 7am-2:30pm & Sun 7am-3pm

FASHION & LIFESTYLE -local labels-

© Elodie Daguin

MAISON KITSUNÉ

52, rue de Richelieu (1st) Ⓜ Bourse / Pyramides
& St-Germain (6th), Oberkampf (11th), Pigalle (9th)

📷 @maisonkitsunestore

Kit-suné, this sounds familiar, doesn't it? If you don't know their creations, you may have heard this name dropped in electro playlists (under acts such as Hot Chip or Two Door Cinema Club). The multifaceted Franco-Japanese house is at once a music and a fashion label. On both fronts, the fox-faced brand (kitsune = fox in Japanese) teams up with international names for cool collabs. Simple and casual designs with a boisterous twist, bold colours and playful patterns are their forte.

🕐 Mon-Sat 11am-7:30pm / Sun 1pm-6:30pm

📞 +33 1 42 60 34 28

MAISON LABICHE

24, rue de Poitou (3rd) Ⓜ Filles du Calvaire

📷 @maisonlabiche

Simplicity is the ultimate sophistication, if the pieces signed by Maison Labiche are anything to go by. Timeless basics that never go out of style. The house's signature is handwritten embroidery, stitched right above the heart, on top quality cotton. Choose whether you are more Mademoiselle, Femme Fatale, Enfant Terrible or Crème de la crème. Else, add your personal touch and customize their tees, sweaters and sailor shirts (the kids' onesies are adorable!) The perfect blend of ancestral savoir-faire and the minimalist, personal trend.

🕐 Mon-Fri 11am-2pm & 3pm-7:30pm
   Sat 11am-7:30pm / Sun 11am-6pm

📞 +33 1 42 78 63 10

HARMONY

1, rue Commines (3rd) Ⓜ Saint-Sébastien - Froissart & Galeries Lafayette (9th)

📷 @harmony_paris

Embodying casual elegance with a Parisian flair, Harmony designs are timeless pieces with a modern touch. Their sleek collections, for men and women, feature minimalist silhouettes and loose cuts that will enchant the low-key fashionistas. That androgynous aura of theirs is seriously cool! Caring for quality and traceability above all, the brand only uses the finest fabrics. If you believe that good basics can last a lifetime, then Harmony is for you.

🕐 Tue-Sat 11:30am-7:30am / Sun 1:30pm-7:30pm
   Closed on Mon

📞 +33 1 42 74 49 13

MAISON CHÂTEAU ROUGE
40bis, rue Myrha (18th) Ⓜ Château Rouge
& Galeries Lafayette (9th)

🅾 @maisonchateaurouge

At the crossroads between couture and street culture, this funky label celebrates its namesake neighbourhood - Château Rouge is this seedy and motley working-class district at the foot of the Montmartre slopes. Playing with codes, Maison Château Rouge honours its African heritage by giving a fresh street-wear twist to traditional wax prints. As local as it gets, they source all fabrics from the textile shops in the Little Africa area. The label is also part of a larger social project, since it's primarily a showcase for an organization that aims to develop entrepreneurship on African soil. For men too.

🕐 Tue-Sat 11am-7pm / Closed on Sun & Mon

JOUR/NÉ
Le Bon Marché (7th), L'Exception (1st)
& Tom Greyhound (3rd)

🅾 @jour_ne

On the Jour/Né catwalks, models wear sneakers and are sized like us. Refreshing, eh? Stylish yet easy-to-wear, the spirited designs by this young label are a dream come true. At once street and chic, feminine and practical, the Jour/Né creations speak for a girl's everyday life. Just like their iconic tee that reads Monday, 7:45am ; Friday 11:15pm... Bold at heart yet low-key in vibe, lady in the head but comfy in the shoes, the Jour/Né silhouettes ooze vintage class and sass. Irresistible.

© Jour/Né

FASHION & LIFESTYLE -CONCEPT STORES-

L'APPARTEMENT SÉZANE
1, rue St Fiacre (2nd) Ⓜ Grands Boulevards

📷 @sezane

Morgane Sézalory is the the darling of all modern Parisians. Inspiring a generation, she's the brain behind Sézane - the first digital fashion brand. Vintage at heart, it celebrates Parisian casual chic. L'Appartement is the airy, homey hangout-showroom where the brand showcases their collections. Drop in, dig in, try on, touch, chill, have a coffee...and go home with your finds right away! A revolution for Sézane fans, accustomed to online buying, limited editions and delivery delays. Awe-inspiring!

🕐 Wed-Sat 11am-8pm / Closed Sun-Tue

MERCI
111, boulevard Beaumarchais (3rd)
Ⓜ Saint-Sébastien - Froissart

📷 @merciparis

Multi-faceted, and probably the coolest store in town! It's housed in a humongous warehouse (once a wallpaper factory), yet homey, with a florist and a used books café opening into a courtyard with their famous red retro auto. The atrium has a rotating stack of edgy objects, and the fashion section is more of a large vintage bazaar. The merry mismatch ranges from unique designer pieces to second-hand stuff. The bonus? It's all sustainable: profits go to a charity.

🕐 Mon-Sat 10am-7:30pm / Closed on Sun

📞 +33 1 42 77 00 33

LA GARCONNIÈRE
40, rue des Petits Carreaux (2nd) Ⓜ Sentier

📷 @la_garconniere_

An ode to masculinity, this handsome space has everything today's dandy needs: vintage watches, natural shave care, hip high-tech, funky boxers, designer eyewear and what not. This first concept store dedicated to gents stocks solid quality basics (French-tailored sailor shirts, knitwear and denim), but also fresh finds such as wooden bowties, miki beanies, tweed braces and square-end knitted ties. The 100% male team scout France and Europe to spot the hottest designers, so you will find something unique!

🕐 Tue-Sat 11am-8pm / Sun 1:30pm-6pm

📞 +33 9 73 68 14 47

FASHION & LIFESTYLE -CONCEPT STORES-

FLEUX

39 Rue Sainte-Croix de la Bretonnerie (4th)
Ⓜ Hotel de Ville / Rambuteau

🅾 @fleuxconceptstore

Fleux is a deco-lover's dream come true. Celebrating design that doesn't take itself seriously, the four stores (all in the same street, each with its own mood) stock some seriously quirky home stuff. Whimsical is the key here, whether it's a croissant pin, a lama mug, a Bambi carpet or an organic cheese DIY kit. Looking for an original gift? You'll find it here!

🌐 Mon-Fri 10:45am-7:30pm / Sat 10:30am-8pm
Sun 1:30pm-7:30pm

📞 +33 1 42 78 27 20

EMPREINTES

5, rue de Picardie (3rd) Ⓜ Temple / Filles du Calvaire

🅾 @empreintesparis

Isn't an object so much more precious when it has a story? Empreintes ('fingerprints', like those left by the people behind the pieces) is the marketplace for all things arts-and-craft. An initiative of the creative art trade guild, it is a showcase for local artists and artisans. The airy four-storey building presents homeware, jewellery, ceramics, and also organic toys and design deco items. Each piece is made in France, unique or limited editions straight from the designer's studio. Visit for extraordinary souvenirs.

🌐 Mon-Sat 11am-7pm / Closed on Sun

📞 +33 1 40 09 53 80

FRENCH TROTTERS

128, rue Vieille du Temple (3rd) Ⓜ Saint-Sébastien - Froissart
& 30, rue de Charonne (11th)

🅾 @frenchtrotters

The two French Trotters behind this brand created a space to share their vision of a contemporary wardrobe that mixes quality designer pieces sourced all over the globe. From Tokyo to Stockholm, they select lesser-known but exciting labels to display alongside local designers' wares and their own French Trotters clothing line. Their two flagship stores extend this philosophy to lifestyle, with some trendy home and bath products, magazines and accessories.

🌐 Tue-Sat 11:30-8pm / Sun 2pm-7pm
Closed on Mon

📞 +33 1 47 00 84 35

L'EXCEPTION

24, rue Berger (1st) Ⓜ Les Halles

🅾 @lexception

Like shopping with a French touch? Here it is! L'Exception gathers under one roof the best homegrown designers. Man or woman, you will find what you're looking for, here. This independent store boasts big names as well as edgy newbies, casual to chic, from jewellery to deco stuff. There is something here for all styles and every pocket.

🌐 Mon-Sat 10am-8pm / Sun 11am-7pm

📞 +33 1 40 39 92 34

SHOP 79

FASHION & LIFESTYLE -LITTLE ONES-

BONTON
82-84, rue de Grenelle (7th) Ⓜ Rue du Bac
& 5, bd des Filles du Calvaire (3rd)

📷 @bonton

Bringing a fresh wave of colours and prints, Bonton makes kids wear more exciting. The label was a pioneer in curating for a hip audience seeking something different. Less traditional than the high-end brands, more sophisticated and spirited than mainstream ones, Bonton is a unique retro-chic line. They twist basic cuts and natural fabrics with a bohemian touch and an original palette. Forget boring baby blue and kitsch gaudy pink, here we pull out mustard, toffee, burgundy, teal and sapphire blue. The first Parisian kids' concept store, Bonton also gathers furniture, vintage-style toys and poetic gifts.

🉐 Mon-Sat 10am-7pm / Closed on Sun   📞 +33 1 44 39 09 20

WOMB
93, rue Réaumur, angle rue Aboukir (2nd) Ⓜ Sentier

📷 @womb_concept

Whether you need gear, home stuff or gifts, welcome to WOMB (World of My Baby). You'll surely find something that tickles your fancy. They have a beautiful and extensive selection, spread over three storeys. The Dutch owner selects the top international designers, so you'll get things you don't find everywhere. Their old school wooden toys and adorable deco items are a fave. But WOMB is much more than a boutique… it's also a space dedicated to millennial mamas and papas, with workshops and yoga, a like-minded community exchanging tips on pretty much everything kid-related.

🉐 Mon 2pm-7pm / Tue-Sat 11am-7pm
Closed on Sun

📞 +33 1 42 36 36 37

FASHION & LIFESTYLE -SHABBY CHIC-

THANX GOD I'M A VIP
10, rue de Lancry (10th) Ⓜ Jacques Bonsergent

📷 @thanxgodimavip

For a wonderful shopping experience and whacky looks
'TGV' is a labour of love mixing funky tunes and even funkier vintage threads. This DJ duo, fond of the two, created a spick-and-span, airy space, neatly set up by colours like a showroom. Boasting of a killer playlist and sofas to lounge in with coffee between fittings, their store is shoppers' bliss! The selection is top-notch, quirky and top quality (no synthetics, only natural fabric).

Ⓚ Mon-Sat 2am-8pm / Sun 2am-7pm

Ⓒ +33 1 42 03 02 09   Ⓢ Fancy Pants

CHEZ MAMIE
73 rue Rochechouart (9th) Ⓜ Anvers
& Mamie Blue: 69, rue de Rochechouart

For Gatsby fans and a tailor-made retro makeover
Brigitte, the cheerful glam lady of the house, styles and advises, alters, designs and recreates pieces, and even holds private hairstyle/make-up sessions. This lover of swing and Hollywood's golden age also provides costumes for films, photo shoots, Gatsby parties and other chic events (items can be rented). The three-storey space looks like a vintage fashion museum, chock-full of gems and a superb hat collection.

Ⓚ Mon & Sat 3pm-8pm
Tue-Fri 11am-1:30pm & 3:30pm-8pm
Closed on Sun

Ⓒ +33 1 42 82 09 98   Ⓢ Fancy Pants

VINTAGE DESIR
32, rue des Rosiers (4th)
Ⓜ Saint-Paul

📷 @vintagedesir

For the budget-conscious
In this cubbyhole of a boutique housed in an old 'coiffeur' (hairdresser shop), you might have to rummage through threads, but you'll always find true bargains, since it's restocked daily with new stuff.

Ⓚ Mon-Sun 11am-9pm

Ⓒ +33 1 40 27 04 98

Ⓢ Dive

TILT VINTAGE
8, rue de Rivoli (4th)
Ⓜ Saint-Paul

📷 @tilt_vintage

For the cool cats, 80's style
This friendly shop stocks casual, unisex stuff: perfectos, bombers, bandanas, funky sweaters, K-ways... and lots of denim! Look in here for an addition that will brighten up your wardrobe!

Ⓚ Mon-Sun 11am-8pm

Ⓒ +33 9 61 32 36 38

Ⓢ Casual Chic

Not to mention...

the eclectic mix of old and new, obscure and renowned, jewellery and knickknacks in the pretty arty boutique **Chinemachine**
100, rue des Martyrs (18th)
Ⓜ Abbesses

📷 @chinemachine

Ⓢ Dive

the one-of-a-kind designer pieces at **Come on Eileen** if you have the patience and expert eye to dig through their massive stock in the tiniest space.
16, rue des Taillandiers (11th)
Ⓜ Bastille

Ⓢ Fancy Pants

the French designer finds (Courèges, Givenchy, Céline) at **Rose Market Vintage**

5, rue Hippolyte Lebas (9th)
Ⓜ Cadet

📷 @rosemarketvintage

Ⓢ Fancy Pants

the top quality pin-up selection from the 30's-50's at **Mamz'Elle Swing**
35 bis, rue du roi de Sicile (4th)
Ⓜ Saint-Paul

Ⓢ Fancy Pants

FASHION & LIFESTYLE -FIFTY SCENTS-

LIQUIDES: LE BAR À PARFUMS
9, rue de Normandie (3rd) Ⓜ Filles du Calvaire

📷 @liquidesbaraparfums

This "perfume bar" is a unique and intimate space where you'll find niche brands and designer fragrances. Taking a stand against marketing-driven corporations, this independent label celebrates creativity and individuality. A list of unknown names on the shelves in a logo-less space is not intimidating, but rather quite refreshing! Find the fragrance that reflects you, from this carefully curated selection.

🕔 Mon-Fri 11am-7:30pm / Sat 11am-8pm
Closed on Sun

📞 +33 9 66 94 77 06

NOSE
20, rue Bauchamont (2nd) Ⓜ Sentier

📷 @noseparis

Finding your signature scent is exciting yet challenging. If you find department stores and beauty shops overwhelming (even underwhelming), head to Nose. Their attentive team run olfactive diagnostics. Answer a few questions, sniff some suggested samples, and receive your fragrance profile and five couture recommendations. The personal attention and beautiful setting make for a pleasant experience. They have hard-to-find perfumes and uncommon designers, plus a wooden scent bar where you can even design your own fragrance.

🕔 Mon-Sat 10:30am-7:30pm / Closed on Sun
📞 +33 1 40 26 46 03

BULY L'OFFICINE UNIVERSELLE 1803
6, rue Bonaparte (6th) Ⓜ Mabillon

📷 @officine_universelle_buly

Feeling nostalgic about those golden days when natural remedies were concocted in rustic apothecaries? This charming cosmetics label takes you back in time. Revisiting traditions and celebrating French artisanal know-how, Buly 1803 recreates stunning interiors - no fake vintage here, everything made 18th-century-style with exquisite wood detail! In this curio-cabinet, you'll find one-of-a-kind products, delicate, quirky and with a fascinating back story, be they combs, scented rocks, rare oils, water-based perfumes bottled in hand-painted porcelain flacons...

🕔 Mon-Sat 10am-7pm / Closed on Sun
📞 +33 1 43 29 02 50

SYNCHROPHONE RECORDS
6, rue des Taillandiers (11th) (M) Ledru-Rollin

(O) @syncrophone

The Parisian reference for all indie electronic music-lovers, Synchrophone has been around for over a decade. Stalwarts in the French house and techno scene, the dream team do a three in one: they guide your digging through their well-stocked shop, which also produces sweet stuff with the house label (think Theo Parrish, Zadig and Voiski) and distributes worldwide, helping export a bunch of cool French labels such as Apollonia, Cracki, D.KO Records, Skylax and many more. Drop in for a chat with Bastien; you might be in for a couple of hours but he'll surely find you fresh gems to bring home!

(★) Tue-Sat 12pm-7:30pm / Closed on Sun & Mon   (C) +33 1 48 05 35 30

BETINO'S RECORD SHOP
32, rue Saint-Sébastien (11th) (M) Oberkampf

(O) @betinosrecordshop

Betino Errera's friendly neighbourhood shop stocks loads of second-hands in mint condition, so head here to unearth some precious original pressings. The expert selection focuses on all things soul, funk, disco, house, jazz and Latin. Kudos to Betino and his crew for the warm and spirited vibes, top service, and not least the eclectic picks! An intensely personal space, launched twenty years ago, Betino's feels like home.

(★) Mon-Sat 1pm-8pm / Closed on Sun

(C) +33 1 43 14 61 34

> **Not to mention...** the reissue label **Superfly Records** and their stellar selection of jazz, funk and soul rarities from all over the world (prominently Brazilian, African and Latin) - @superfly.records

ARTS & CRAFTS

AFWOSH

10, rue d'Hauteville (10th) Ⓜ Bonne Nouvelle

 @afwosh

Afterworkshop - here's a peculiar name! A magic word just as peculiar as the merry mishmash filling this boutique: zany gadgets, funky jewellery, pretty purses, hip-tech gear, designer clothes, stationery and other knick-knacks at sweet prices. The collection caters to men, women, kids (...and inner children!), with many Parisian labels and also some Scandinavian finds. In short, the dream spot to find a cool gift, with the fun vibes of an after-work retail therapy.

🕸 Mon-Sat 11am-8pm / Closed on Sun

📞 +33 9 52 91 44 80

BAZARTHERAPY

15, rue Beaurepaire (10th) Ⓜ Jacques Bonsergent

📷 @bazartherapy

If you are one for surprises, swing by this gift den, and you'll find something you didn't really need but desperately want. This modern-day bazaar celebrates the weird and wonderful through an eclectic mix of original creations and little objects picked up from quirky designers. Return to kid mode, and step into their fantasy world. Spirited souvenirs and fun vibes await. Their treat cones will steal your heart! Else, create your own lucky bag with PEZ candy dispensers and epic retro treasures.

🕸 Tue-Sat 11am-7:30pm / Sun 2pm-7pm
Closed on Mon

📞 +33 1 42 40 10 11

PAPIER TIGRE

5, rue des Filles du Calvaire (3rd) Ⓜ Filles du Calvaire & Artazart (10th), Le Bon Marché (7th)

📷 @papiertigram

Behind this cheerful tiger's-head label hide a bunch of creative folks who like to play with paper. Fold, colour, twist it with funky patterns. Their store and lab in the hip Upper-Marais is a playground for those who still swear by pencils and rulers, send cards or take handwritten notes. What's certain is that Papier Tigre will illuminate any prim desk, boring list or serious assignment. But their colourful creations go beyond stationery, so curious minds will delight in the toys, accessories and house stuff.

🕸 Mon-Fri 11:30am-7:30pm / Sat 11am-8pm
Closed on Sun

📞 +33 1 48 04 00 21

ARTAZART
83, quai de Valmy (10th) Ⓜ Jacques Bonsergent

◎ @artazart83

Along the Canal Saint Martin, a bright orange storefront beckons. It hides a bookshop that's established as a reference point for all art buffs and pros. Magazines and books on architecture, web design, photo, cinema, street art and what not, this place celebrates all things visual. Expect also a range of nerdy knick-knacks, gifts and funky children's books.

🗱 Mon-Fri 10:30am-7:30pm / Sat 11am-7:30pm
Sun 1pm-7:30pm

☎ +33 1 40 40 24 03

OFR.
20, rue Dupetit-Thouars (3rd) Ⓜ Temple

◎ @ofrparis

Fashion and design-lovers will fall for this one! The eclectic selection of this edgy bookstore is a treat to dig into: arty postcards, fanzines, fashion accessories from obscure designers, photo books, but also antique hardbacks. They are known as the local expert in indie magazines (contemporary art and fashion), mostly in English. You'll find niche publications you've never even heard of! They also host exhibitions of young artists from various horizons.

🗱 Mon-Sat 10am-8pm / Sun 2pm-7pm

☎ +33 1 42 45 72 88

LE MONTE EN L'AIR
2, rue de la Mare (20th) Ⓜ Ménilmontant

◎ @aurelie.montenlair

This quirky shop perched atop the Belleville hill is a favourite with book-lovers. A gem of an indie bookstore, it delights in showing off alternative stuff: a massive amount of graphic works (novels, comics...), some obscure, weird and political titles, but also poetry and exciting kids' books. There is always something sweet happening here, whether it's a book launch, a concert, an illustration exhibit or a meet-and-greet with authors. Come hang out; their café and terrace are lovely to while away the hours!

🗱 Mon-Fri 1pm-8pm / Sat 10am-8pm
Sun 1pm-8pm

☎ +33 1 40 22 04 54

TASCHEN BOOKSTORE
2, rue de Buci (6th) Ⓜ Odéon / Mabillon

◎ @taschen

German publisher Taschen has some seriously cool stuff up its sleeve. Like that collection of funk and soul covers, the XL edition of Helmut Newtown's work or the A-Z history of the Bauhaus. Specializing in art and design, it also stocks some travel and kinky books. In these sleek, Parisian interiors, amid over-sized volumes on display, pick up coffee table books to gift to your arty friends, or indulge yourself!

🗱 Mon-Sun 11am-8pm

☎ +33 1 40 51 79 22

FONDATION VUITTON
@freeaparis

GET
ARTSY

VISUAL ARTS

© Georges Meguerditchian

CENTRE POMPIDOU

Place Georges-Pompidou (4th) (M) Rambuteau / Hôtel de Ville

(O) @centrepompidou

At first look, it seems like a maze of tubes and pipes. But once you get the colour code, it all starts to make sense: blue is for circulating air, yellow for electricity, green for water and red for people. This glass and steel structure houses an airy cultural space that was ground-breaking when erected in the late 1970s. The Beaubourg Museum of Modern Art was a futuristic architectural alien back then. If the building is not as edgy today, it remains cool. The art is thought-provoking, and the blockbuster exhibitions are always a hit. Plus, the view from the top is wow and the plaza a great place to people-watch and check out some street art. Pre-book tickets to skip the queues.

(⏰) Wed-Mon 11am-9pm / Thu till 11pm / Closed on Tue   (☎) +33 1 44 78 12 33   (⑤) €14

© Iwan Baan

FONDATION LOUIS VUITTON

8, avenue du Mahatma Gandhi, Bois de Boulogne (16th) (M) Sablons

(O) @fondationlv

Since sprouting in the Bois de Boulogne in 2014, this place has never ceased to amaze. The Louis Vuitton foundation is an architectural sensation that took things Parisian to another level. This masterpiece of a building designed by American architect Frank Gehry is worth a visit in itself. Twelve curved panels of glass delicately render the feel of windblown sails in a unique way. The contemporary art collection is engaging, and the panoramic views are the icing on the cake. Heads-up: you have to earn this! Buy tickets online, but be prepared to wait anyway. Also note that it's a little out of the way in the forest (a ten-minute walk from the nearest transportation).

(⏰) Mon-Thu 11am-8pm / Fri 11am-9pm   (☎) +33 1 40 69 96 00   (⑤) €16
Sat-Sun 9am-11pm / Closed on Tue

PALAIS DE TOKYO
13, avenue du Président Wilson (16th)
Ⓜ Trocadéro

🅾 @palaisdetokyo

Of palace, it has only the name. This anti-museum may be housed in a rather royal building; it's actually a vast wasteland inside, where the weird and wonderful have a field day. Ballsy and edgy, this one-of-a-kind exhibition space is where the cool is. With monumental installations, memorable performances and carte blanche, the Palais de Tokyo has to be the most exciting spot in the Parisian cultural sphere! If you're one for art that pushes, disturbs and challenges, drop in!

✪ Wed-Mon 12pm-12am / Closed on Tue

☏ +33 1 81 97 35 88   💲 €12

INSTITUT DU MONDE ARABE
1, rue des Fossés Saint-Bernard (5th)
Ⓜ Jussieu / Cardinal Lemoine

🅾 @institutdumondearabe

France and the Arab world have a history that goes a long way back. Legit then to showcase the Arab civilisation in a place of its own. Sitting elegantly on the banks of the Seine River, the immaculate facade of the IMA – designed by star French architect Jean Nouvel – is incrusted with 240 lattice windows following the sun and adjusting to light. The museum houses an extensive collection (from textile and ceramics to calligraphy and contemporary art), a teahouse and a rooftop with a fab view.

✪ Tue-Fri 10am-6pm / Sat-Sun 10am-7pm / Closed on Mon

☏ +33 1 40 51 38 38   💲 €8 / 4€ - 26 y/o

MAISON EUROPÉENNE DE LA PHOTOGRAPHIE
5/7, rue de Fourcy (4th)
Ⓜ Saint-Paul / Pont Marie / Hôtel de Ville

🅾 @mep_paris

If you are a photo buff, you'll have a blast at MEP! This vast gallery space, housed in an elegant hôtel particulier in the Marais, offers space to the world's most exciting contemporary photographers. The permanent collections feature influential masters such as Raymond Depardon, Irving Penn and Martin Parr, while the temporary exhibits include photojournalism, fashion and art photography, or retrospectives.

✪ Wed-Sun 11am-7:45pm / Closed on Mon & Tue

☏ +33 1 44 78 75 00   💲 9€

FONDATION CARTIER
261, bd Raspail (14th)
Ⓜ Raspail / Denfert Rochereau

🅾 @fondationcartier

The stunning glass building and gorgeous garden of the Cartier Foundation for Contemporary Art constitute works of art in themselves. Check out what's on; they do have some really cool stuff scheduled in the photo, video and fashion department, as well as some special events known as Nomadic Nights (talks, music and dance sessions, workshops and kids' activities) to continue the fun of the exhibition.

✪ Tue-Sun 11am-8pm (till 10pm on Tue) / Closed on Mon

☏ +33 1 42 18 56 50   💲 €10,50 / Reduced rate: €7

VISUAL ARTS

MUSÉE RODIN

77, rue de Varenne (7th) (M) Varenne / Invalides

(O) @museerodinparis

The evocative intensity and delicate beauty of Rodin's works made him the father of modern sculpture and a Parisian legend to remember. The magnificent Hôtel Biron celebrates his genius. In keeping with Rodin's philosophy, the place sets nature as the frame for sculpture. Stroll through the monumental garden and spot some iconic works, such as The Thinker. With the Eiffel Tower in sight, the rose garden, loads of nooks and crannies to explore, it's an exquisite experience.

Tue-Sun 10am-5:45pm / Closed on Mon

+33 1 44 18 61 10 10€

PETIT PALAIS

Avenue Winston Churchill (8th)
(M) Champs-Élysées Clémenceau

(O) @petitpalais_musee

This architectural gem was erected for the 1900 Universal Exhibition. Smaller than the Grand Palais only in size, this grand building houses the Fine Arts museum. The permanent collection has works by influential French artists of the 19th century, but honestly, the palace is the true masterpiece! The marble, wrought iron work, floor mosaics and painted ceilings are stunning. Don't miss the inner gardens and the cafe nestled in the colonnade!

Tue-Sun 10am-6pm / Closed on Mon

+33 1 53 43 40 00 €11

MUSÉE PICASSO

5, rue de Thorigny (3rd) (M) Saint-Paul / Chemin Vert

(O) @museepicassoparis

Housed in the beautiful private hotel Salé, this museum brings together elegant 17th-century architecture and the extravagance of the Spanish master. The extensive collection navigates through the different art forms embraced by Picasso (painting, drawing, engraving, photo, film…), painting a quite different picture of the artist. With its fab central staircase, the museum is a treat even if you are not a Picasso aficionado.

Tue-Fri 10:30am-6pm / Sat-Sun 9:30am-6pm
Closed on Mon

+33 1 85 56 00 36 12.50€

PERFORMING ARTS -MULTITASKING SPOTS-

© Jerome Brody

© Yann Kgbeur

POINT ÉPHÉMÈRE
200, quai de Valmy (10th) (M) Jaurès / Louis Blanc

(O) @pointephemere

Along the Canal Saint-Martin, hidden below street level, lies a gem of an alternative venue. Concrete, graffiti covered walls, outdoors by the water, plastic cups, tiny backroom with a sweaty dance-floor... you know, refreshingly low-key. Resident in the old docks, this « ephemeral » arty squat was such a hit back in 2004 that it turned permanent, and became the laidback den of a cool crowd. An incubator, it has artists in residence and hosts a bunch of sweet stuff: exhibitions, dance and theatre performances, talks, workshops, charity events... plus dope DJ sets and indie gigs!

(K) Mon-Sun 12:30pm-2am (till 10pm on Sun)   (C) +33 1 40 34 04 06

© Pascal Montary

© Pascal Montary

À LA FOLIE
26, av. Corentin Cariou (19th) (M) Corentin Cariou

(O) @alafolie.paris

Set in the Parc de la Villette, à la folie is a living space to meet, mingle and chill. With its garden opening on the park, three terraces, barbecue by the canal de l'Ourcq and massive communal picnic table, it's a hybrid of a place, fit to linger in any time of day. Play Ping-Pong or pétanque outside, retro arcade games inside or lounge in the psychedelic-painted room. à la folie has something for everyone – DJ sets, art workshops, vinyl diggers' nights, kid stuff, yoga classes. The music line up is top-notch (with an ex from the REX at the helm).

(K) Mon-Thu 12pm-12am / Fri-Sun 12pm-2am   (C) +33 7 76 79 70 66

PERFORMING ARTS -LIVE MUSIC-

LA BELLEVILLOISE
19-21, rue Boyer (20th) Ⓜ Ménilmontant
◎ @labellevilloise

This pretty edifice, in the heart of working-class Belleville district, was Paris's first-ever workers co-op. The industrial feel was retained and the place turned into a fiercely indie cultural venue where you wine, dine, dance and unwind. In the lofty inner garden, under age-old olive trees, relish jazz-lulled brunch on Sundays or savour acoustic concerts on weekdays. There's also a club, a bar, a space for markets, exhibitions and festivals plus a terrace, which is the dream hangout when sunny days return.

🕃 Wed-Thu 7pm-1am / Fri-Sat 7pm-6am / Sun 11:30am-4pm & 7pm-1am   ☎ +33 1 46 36 07 07
Closed on Mon & Tue

© W. Beaucardet   © W. Beaucardet

LA PHILARMONIE DE PARIS
221, avenue Jean Jaurès (19th) Ⓜ Porte de Pantin
◎ @philharmoniedeparis

Another architectural odd ship signed by Jean Nouvel, The Philarmonie is a place dedicated to fine music in all forms. First and foremost a concert hall, with a line up ranging from classic to jazz with detours through world music, it is also a museum, a media library and a venue for music-related events. Standing in the Parc de la Villette, a cool culture and entertainment spot at the east of the city, it boasts interiors that are optimum for super sound and a fantastic listening experience.

☎ +33 1 44 84 44 84

PERFORMING ARTS -LIVE MUSIC-

NEW MORNING
7 & 9, rue des Petites Ecuries (10th) (M) Château d'Eau

(O) @newmorningparis

Prince had made it his Parisian home for epic wild jams. And literally every single jazz, blues, and folk figure you can think of has played in this tiny club – Chet Baker, Nina Simone, Archie Shepp, Betty Carter... It doesn't look like much, really just a blank space with no deco. Not very comfy. But it's oh-so-cosy! Surrounding the stage, the audience are as close as they can get to the artists, making for a very special moment. Unassuming not only in appearance, the New Morning also has a no-fuss attitude. Elegance doesn't need showing off here. The focus is the music, only the music.

LA MAROQUINERIE
23, rue Boyer (20th) (M) Ménilmontant

(O) @lamaroquinerie

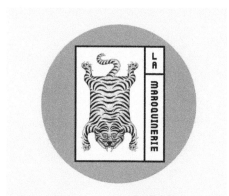

For a good old indie gig, this intimate venue is a must. Set in an old leather factory, the friendly place promises a killer concert experience (with artists usually in for a chat with the audience). It's always packed and pumping, but thanks to the multi-level setting, the stage remains visible to everyone. It is hot and sweaty, but that's part of the fun! The key here is the sound – amazing! – and the neat eclectic programming. The upstairs bar and courtyard restaurant are great to start the night.

(K) Mon-Sun 6pm-2am

(C) +33 1 40 33 35 05

LA MÉCANIQUE ONDULATOIRE
8, Passage Thiéré (11th)
(M) Bréguet-Sabin / Bastille / Ledru-Rollin

(O) @lamecaniqueondulatoire

A haunt of true rock fans, this venue is as local, authentic and underground as it gets!
A retro bar upstairs to chill, and a basement cave for some dirty rock, punk and metal gig have made it a much-loved hangout. It's a bit seedy but welcoming, and beautiful in its own, raw way. The spirited line up brings to the fore niche discoveries, while the cool crew make it a super personal place. An indie haven, which sadly has just been forced to ramp down the live gigs. Thankfully, the bar is still in place, vibrating with their legendary vinyl DJ sets.

(K) Mon-Sun 6pm-2am

(C) +33 1 43 55 69 14

PERFORMING ARTS -FESTIVALS-

PARIS FACE CACHÉE

SIESTES ÉLECTRONIQUES

FÊTE DE LA MUSIQUE
© Amélie Dupont - Paris Tourist Office

PARIS L'ÉTÉ

PARIS FACE CACHÉE
 @parisfacecachee   1rst weekend of Feb.

Get in behind the scenes and discover the secrets of Paris! Play urban explorers, with unique activities (some after dark) in exciting locations: abandoned factories and hospitals, private mansions, secret gardens, restricted libraries, and airports... Whether arty discoveries, innovative green initiatives, foodie delights, or hidden heritage gems, you're up for some great adventures!
Some visits and workshops cost a few euros but most are free. First come, first serve, so be an early bird and register online in Jan.

MUSIC FESTIVALS
@thepeacocksociety, @lessiestes, @rockenseine, @weatherfestival

• **Peacock Society** (Feb. & July): An exciting mix of big names and new talent, warehouse and green space; a weekend of gritty techno in the Parc Floral de Vincennes.
• **Paris Jazz Festival** (June-July): A stellar line-up, summer nights, picnics in the botanical gardens, and free live jazz make for exquisite times.
• **Siestes Électroniques** (1rst weekend of July): Experimental electro at the Musée du Quai Branly; this original event allows DJs to explore the museum's audio stock, which is overflowing with world musical gems. It's all free – get your invite in June from www.quaibranly.fr
• **Rock en Seine** (late August): Three days of rock and more in the heritage-listed park of the Domaine de St-Cloud.
• **Weather Festival** (June & Oct.): The finest underground house and techno, brought to you by the Concrète dream team at the edgy Bourget airport.

WE LOVE GREEN
 @welovegreen   1rst weekend of June

Not just a music fest, WLG is an initiative that gets it all on point! The 100% sustainable party, held in a forest, comes up innovative ways to reduce our footprint. The spirited event is also a environmental lab but doesn't take itself too seriously. It boasts of an exceptional, eclectic line-up and irresistible feel-good vibes, definitely the coolest festival in town.

WEATHER
@jacobkhrist

WE LOVE GREEN

CINEMA MAC MAHON
LOST IN FRENCHLATION AND LIDF PRESENT
FLANEURS

LOST IN FRENCHLATION

NUIT BLANCHE
© Sophie Robichon / Paris Tourist Office

FÊTE DE LA MUSIQUE   @fetemusique   June 21rst
All genres, all venues; from amateur jams to huge gigs, choirs, and marching bands; in squares, courtyards, museums, and even train stations... Music takes over the whole city (rather country). The huge street fest spreads across all public areas and is completely free. Wander the streets and join in the party anywhere!

PARIS L'ÉTÉ   @parislete   Mid-July - early Aug.
"Arts, scenes, and sun"; here's the kind of program we love! Through the summer months, the performing arts take a field trip and enliven the city's parks, castles, courtyards, museums, and even historic school buildings. The lucky folks who skipped the beach can attend gigs, plays, and dance and circus shows in a unique setting, all for free or next to nothing. (Book from June on parislete.fr)

LOST IN FRENCHLATION   @lostinfrenchlation   Year-long
Love French cinema, but no mastery of the language? These special screenings bring to you the classics and the latest releases with English subtitles. Oui, oui! The Parisian charm is kept intact with the setting being in those old indie theatres.

NUIT BLANCHE   @quefaireaparis   1rst weekend of Oct.
"White Night" (read "all-nighter") is one of its kind. Art takes the streets of Paris by storm for two nights, with outdoor installations and performances blossoming in unusual places. Also, if you dream of a night at the museum, this is your chance; most cultural spots stay open after dark.

LA BELLEVILLOISE

NIGHT-
OWLING

NEIGHBOURHOOD BARS

LES NIÇOIS

7, rue Lacharrière (11th)
(M) Saint-Ambroise / Rue Saint Maur

(O) @lesnicois

Bringing a slice of Mediterranean *joie de vivre* to Paris, this gastropub celebrates its city of origin: Nice. Come share some tapas, washed down with a bottle of rosé, play pétanque, and chill like it's a weekend on the French Riviera. Friendly vibes. The lunch set is a dope deal.

Go for... the iconic *pan bagnat* (a super sandwich) and *pissaladière* (a thin onion and anchovy tart). On the liquid front, the star Ricard is a must-have.

Mon-Sat 12am-2pm / Sun 11:30am-5pm

+33 9 84 16 55 03

KIEZ BIERGARTEN

24, rue Vauvenargues (18th) (M) Guy Môquet
& Kiez Kanal (19th)

(O) @kiezbiergarten

"Kiez" is the hood for German folks. And so, the beer garden hidden behind this Montmartre bistro exudes this uber-friendly Oktoberfest no-fuss fun. In the kitchen, everything is hausgemacht (read homemade) and hearty. It's a laidback spot to chill during the day that bustles in the evening.

Go for... a Curry wurzt, a warm pretzel, and a pint of Paulaner Hefe (or a Club Mate, if on booze detox).

Mon-Sun 10am-2am

+33 1 46 27 78 46

AUX DEUX AMIS

45, rue Oberkampf (11th) (M) Oberkampf

A long-running and much-loved institution, this tiny bar serves terrific tapas. The *menu du jour* is displayed on an age-old neon-lit mirror. The retro deco and no-fuss pulsing ambience are irresistible. It's always packed, but that's part of the charm! Squeeze in at the counter and soak in the infectious Parisian bistro vibe. Late-night drop-ins are also good fun.

Go for... the spot-on jamon and natural wines.

Tue-Fri 9:30am-2am / Sat 12pm-2am
Closed on Sun & Mon

+33 1 58 30 38 13

LE COEUR FOU

rue Montmarte (2nd) (M) Sentier

On a busy pedestrian street, at the heart of hyper-gentrified Montorgueil, this tiny cocktail bar is a find; a neighbourhood joint since 1997. It has retained its authentic "village" vibe. Casual and friendly, it has more charm than the average around (candle-lit nooks and an old wooden counter). The music is always on point. On summer days, the tables spill out onto the street for an apéro in the sun.

Go for... a caipirinha or a mojito.

Mon-Sun 5pm-2am

+33 1 42 33 04 98

VIGNES
76, bd de la Villette (19th) (M) Colonel Fabien / Belleville

(O) @vigneslebaravin

VIGNES — it's wine au naturel. Boasting a curated selection of biodynamic wines, the cave a manger also serves up fresh plates and planches with A1 artisanal goodies. The funky trio behind VIGNES guides you expertly yet unpretentiously, always keen on sharing their finds, pairing these with great vibes (lots of smile and some DJ sets on special occasions). And when the sun comes out, the terrace is a lovely hangout.

🍷 Go for... *the planche mixte* and the organic Chausey oysters.

⚡ Wed-Thur 11am-2pm & 5pm-11pm / Fri 11am-2pm & 5pm-12am   📞 +33 1 44 52 96 53
Sat 11am-12am / Closed on Sun & Mon

CHEZ GEORGES
11, rue des Canettes (6th) (M) Mabillon

This timeless red storefront houses a legendary institution. Under the stone vaults of this tiny cellar, lies the soul of Saint-Germain. Squeeze in at the counter or at the nooks and crannies of the top floor for a drink or two, but get down to the basement, and the kitsch retro playlist will draw you in for a sweaty dance session. The crowd is a colourful bunch, the place authentic to bits, the vibe ever-festive and friendly; it feels like family.

⚡ Sun & Mon 6pm-1am / Tue-Sat 6pm-2am
(cave opens at 8pm)

📞 +33 1 43 26 79 15

MONSIEUR MATTHIEU
101, rue du Chemin Vert (11th) (M) Rue Saint-Maur

MM, nicknamed by its regulars, has a couple of cool things to pull out: killer planches, artisanal treats from small producers, wines at sweet prices, and a top-of-the-game team.

The no-fuss bar really feels like home, especially the basement with its retro deco and living room vibe. You can bring your gang and make it yours. BYO music applies.

🍷 Go for... the *rillettes* and the *planche mixte* (the chive butter pulls back the crowds).

⚡ Tue & Wed 6pm-12am / Thu-Sat 6pm-2am
Closed on Sun & Mon

📞 +33 1 84 06 50 95

NEIGHBOURHOOD BARS -VINTAGE VIBES-

LE COMPTOIR GÉNÉRAL
80, quai de Jemmapes (10th) (M) Jacques Bonsergent

(O) @lecomptoirgeneral

Tucked away behind a gate with no sign, this quirky place is so awesome you'll be glad you stepped in, for it's easy to miss. It's the type of huge alternative space you'd find in Berlin or Budapest, but one of its kind in Paris! A cabinet of curios, Le Comptoir is a happy mix of shabby-chic drinking den, tropical garden, African bric-a-brac, and urban wonderland. Come chill and chat to Afro and Latino beats, but drop in early or be ready to wait.

🍸 Go for... the Secousse (vodka, bissap, passion fruit, cucumber).

🍸 Mon-Thu 6pm-2am / Fri 4pm-2am / Sat-Sun 2pm-2am   ☎ +33 1 44 88 24 48   💲 Casual Chic

LE FANTÔME
36, rue de Paradis (10th) (M) Poissonnière

(O) @lefantomeparis

Always dreamt of a little Pacman game from the good ol' days? This joint is for you. Digging out vintage video games, this cheerful bar is a blast from the past. Join in for a flipper game and a beer with the young folks. There is a mini club in the basement, reverberating the 90's jams. Do book a table, for it can get pretty busy.

🍸 Go for... the pizzas.

🍸 Tue-Fri 11am-2am / Sat 6pm-2am
Sun 12pm 3:30pm / Closed on Mon

☎ +33 9 66 87 11 20   💲 Casual Chic

MARLUSSE ET LAPIN
14, rue Germain Pilon (18th) (M) Pigalle

Hidden among Pigalle sex shops, this tiny crazy place must be one of the quirkiest drinking dens in town. Pass the front bar and you'll find yourself in, well, a granny's bedroom! The whole package – flowery wallpaper, B&W photos of ancestors, a massive wooden wardrobe. Sit on the bed, at the dressing table or even in the bathtub, and sip on a little absinthe. Funky cocktails and the cheapest pint around are also on the menu.

🍸 Mon-Sun 6pm-2am

☎ +33 1 42 59 17 97   💲 Dive

NEIGHBOURHOOD BARS -ALFRESCO-

ROSA BONHEUR

Parc des Buttes Chaumont 2, Allée de la Cascade (19th)
Ⓜ Botzaris & Rosa Seine (7th, Invalides)

Ⓞ @rosabonheurofficiel

This modern-day *guinguette* brings back the cheerful and rustic spirit of the working-class open-air dances held in suburbs and small towns in the 19th century. The Rosa nights indeed exude a delightful retro vibe and a touch of the countryside holiday feeling. Rosa Bonheur, the original, is a lodge under the Buttes Chaumont trees, alive with music, dancing, cinema, sports, and kid's stuff. On the banks of the Seine River, a barge called Rosa Bonheur sur Seine is also moored for fun times. Swing by for apéro!

� Thu & Fri 12pm 12am / Sat-Sun 10am-12am
Closed on Mon-Wed

☏ +33 1 48 06 18 48

LE PERCHOIR

14, rue Crespin du Gast (11th) Ⓜ Ménilmontant
& Hôtel de Ville (4th), Gare de l'Est (10th)

Ⓞ @leperchoir

Let's be honest, rooftops are usually a tad fancy and/or touristy. But this one is a true local and casual hangout. Nestled atop Parisian buildings, the Perchoir terraces have a chill vibe. The one in Le Marais (which requires patience to get in) is an unfailing hit, with its unrivalled view, but the Ménilmontant one really steals the show. With Montmartre in the backdrop, a vaster playground, a more alternative vibe, a restaurant, and lots of cool activities happening all year long, it's the real deal!

� Tue-Fri 6pm-2am / Sat 4pm-2am
Closed on Sun & Mon

☏ +33 1 48 06 18 48

LA ROTONDE
(LE GRAND MARCHÉ STALINGRAD)

6-8, place de la Bataille Stalingrad (19th) Ⓜ Jaurès

Ⓞ @grandmarchestalingrad

Remnants of the wall that marked the limits of inner-city Paris, the historical building of La Rotonde has been brought to a funkier second life. This grand edifice is now a multipurpose venue and the gem of this regenerating neighbourhood. The mini club hiding under the dome regularly features cool local DJ collectives, so keep an ear out! The outside is a green zone with food stalls, plenty of space to chill by the canal, and a greenhouse.

� Sun-Thu 10am-11pm / Fri-Sat 10am-6am

☏ +33 1 80 48 33 40

COCKTAIL DENS - STELLAR SPEAKEASIES -

© Steven Reti

EXPERIMENTAL COCKTAIL CLUB
37, rue Saint-Sauveur (2nd) Ⓜ Sentier
& Prescription Cocktail Club (6th)

📷 @experimentalevents

Ten years and the mixology den created by the expert Experimental Group - pioneer of the Parisian speakeasy – hasn't aged a day! It has a cosy and intimate feel, with a sweet soundtrack and pleasant volume levels. But what truly hits the spot are the concoctions. Restyled with rare spirits, fresh fruits, and delicate special touches, they keep daring and changing but never disappoint. The muted weekday mood leads to a packed and bustling weekend bar.

🕹 Mon-Thu 7pm-2am / Fri-Sat 7pm-4am
Sun 8pm-2am

📞 +33 1 45 08 88 09

HARRY'S NEW YORK BAR
5, rue Daunou (2nd) Ⓜ Opéra

📷 @harrysnewyorkbar

Wanna feel like an 'American in Paris'? Step into this legendary venue where Hemingway used to hang out and the Bloody Mary was created. It's as authentic as it gets, as the owner imported original bar deco straight from Manhattan in 1911. Come sip one of the bartenders' creations in the basement piano bar to the sound of live jazz. Otherwise, the upstairs room has more of a good old-school pub vibe with a long list of whiskies and beers.

🕹 Mon-Sat 12pm-2pm / Sun 4pm-1am

📞 +33 1 42 61 71 14

LE MARY CÉLESTE
1, rue Commines (3rd) Ⓜ Filles du Calvaire

📷 @lemaryceleste

The exposed bricks and central circular bar grant Mary Céleste the feel of a casual neighbourhood bar, but a glam touch raises the bar. There's an oyster counter and some pretty fine small plates to nibble along with your killer cocktails. A word to the wise, come early or book ahead so you can sit at the main bar upstairs.

🍽 Go for... the Rain Dog. Food-wise, the devilled egg and the veal tartare are sensational.

🕹 Mon-Sun 6pm-2am

📞 +33 9 80 72 98 83

© Silvere Koulouris

LE TRÈS PARTICULIER
23, avenue Junot (18th) (M) Lamarck-Caulaincourt

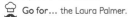 @tresparticulier

In a Montmartre private lane, tucked away behind metal gates, this mansion houses the most stunning and exclusive hotel in Paris. Its lush garden is a magical place where time stands still, and nature reigns supreme in all its glory. The secluded venue opens its bar to cocktail-lovers in the know. It's an intimate boudoir extending to a greenhouse, with a dose of the very kitsch-cool Twin Peaks touch. The ambiance is chic obviously, yet never stiff, with DJ sets most nights of the week. To spot it, you'll need a solid GPS, as even locals have trouble finding it, but that's part of the charm!

🍴 **Go for...** the Laura Palmer.

P.S. If you are not the cocktail type, yet want to check out this one-of-a-kind place, L'Hôtel Particulier also has a teahouse. So, join in for Sunday brunch or afternoon tea under the trees.

🕐 Mon-Sun 6pm-2am   📞 +33 1 53 41 81 40

© Jefferson Lellouche

© Shehan Hanwellage

COCKTAIL DENS -EXOTIC TREATS-

DIRTY DICK
10, rue Frochot (9th) Ⓜ Pigalle

📷 @dirtydickparis

Behind an obscure shop-front that might seem shut down (formerly a hostess bar, hence the cheeky name), you'll find a funky tiki bar that concocts outstanding cocktails. Fruit and rum-based, the creations are all crafted with care. But, with the brilliant mixology level, the no-fuss attitude is equally present. The vibe is chill, the music on point, and the staff super friendly and fun. Sit back on a cane chair and enjoy the ride!

❇ Mon-Sun 6pm-2am

☎ +33 1 48 78 74 58

LA MEZCALERIA
1K Hotel 13, bd du Temple (3rd) Ⓜ Filles du Calvaire

📷 @lamezcaleriaparis

This clandestino bar hides behind the kitchens of the adjacent Peruvian restaurant in the 1K hotel. Push through the white door, and you'll find yourself immersed in a bright Dio de los Muertos decor. Not kitsch, though, but quite cool. This Mexican speakeasy gives top billing to *mezcal*, the star spirit cousin of tequila. Served neat as shots or in spirited cocktails, they are all artisanal and imported.

😋 Go for... the glorious guacamole.

❇ Mon-Fri 6pm-2am / Sat 6pm-3am
Closed on Sun & Mon

☎ +33 1 42 71 20 00

CANDELERIA
52, rue de Saintonge (3rd) Ⓜ Filles du Calvaire

📷 @candelariaparis

In this compact Mexican joint, you can devour delish tacos and tapas, but the secret lies behind the random white door at the back of the taqueria. Here, you can access a hidden bar that shakes up world-class agave-based cocktails.

😋 Go for... the Guêpe Verte, a refreshing mix of tequila, agave, lime, coriander, and cucumber, lifted with a little chilli.

❇ Mon-Sun 12pm-2am

☎ +33 1 42 74 41 28

© Fabien Voileau

L'ENTRÉE DES ARTISTES
30, rue Victor Massé (9th) Ⓜ Pigalle

Ⓞ @entreedesartistespigalle

This sweet spot is perfect to kick off the night! The subtle lights, brick walls, and vintage deco create a warm and cosy ambience. Neat tapas and cocktails are on the menu of this elegant bar. Things are kept casual, although with a groovy soundtrack. Modern soul, rare disco, jazz funk, and Brazilian beats, all on vinyl only. Their BOTTLE parties are the bomb, graced by guests such as Marcellus Pittman, Floating Points, or Pablo Valentino.

🍽 Go for... the cocktails (Carlos or Mon Vieux Tabac) and the Spanish beef ham.

🕑 Tue-Thu 7:30pm-2am / Fri-Sat 7:30pm-5am / Closed on Sun & Mon

📞 +33 1 45 23 11 93   Ⓢ Casual Chic

DJOON
22, boulevard Vincent Auriol (12th) Ⓜ Quai de la Gare

Ⓞ @djoonclub

DJOON is of those happy, no-nonsense spots for dancers and music-lovers. The intimate NY-style club was the pioneer in the afro-house sound, inviting Detroit/Chicago legends to debut in France, teaming up with African DJs, and throwing epic Motown parties. The crowd is eclectic and forward-thinking (thirty-somethings mostly). Behind the decks, expect world guests, emerging and big names alike. Don't be an early bird, the dancefloor comes alive by 1:30am!

🕑 Wed-Thu 5pm-12am / Fri 5pm-5am   Ⓢ €10
Sat 11pm-5am

PARTY JOINTS -LIVE LEGENDS-

© Virgil Gesbert

CONCRÈTE
Port de la Rapée (12th) Ⓜ Gare de Lyon

Ⓞ @concrete.paris

La Concrète, as connoisseurs call it, is the go-to place for electro aficionados. This barge, moored on the Austerlitz bank, started off as a daytime after-party, transforming into the first Parisian round-the-clock club. Their Samedimanches ('Satundays', read party marathons where nights turn into days) are legendary, just like their line-up – the very best of techno and house, both locally and internationally. Their outdoor Woodfloor is fab for dancing the weekend away. When the sun rises over the Seine River and the music kicks in, it's a bit of magic!

🎧 Fri-Sat 10pm-10am / Samedimanche Sat 10pm - Mon 2am   €15

© Alban Gendrot

REX CLUB
5, bd Poissonnière (2nd) Ⓜ Bonne Nouvelle

Ⓞ @rexclub

Alive and kicking since the early 90's, the Parisian temple of techno doesn't look a day older. Located in the basement of the Art Deco REX cinema, this iconic venue started by local legend Laurent Garnier, hasn't lost any of its opening glory. At the front line of the acid house revolution, it remains to date the prime party spot for the underground scene, boasting an unrivalled sound system and a stellar line-up. The same pro crowd and beautiful vibes, then and now, is what makes it special.

🎧 Thu-Sat 11:30pm/12am-7am   📞 +33 1 42 36 10 96   💲 €7-17

PARTY JOINTS -LIVE LEGENDS-

LA JAVA

105, rue du Faubourg du Temple (10th) Ⓜ Belleville

📷 @lajavabelleville

This iconic dance-hall, hidden in the basement of an Art-Deco arcade, was home to the *zazous* – those funky Parisian kids mad about swing in the 1940's. Rocked by accordion notes, the centennial place saw Édith Piaf debut and Django Reinhardt's first gypsy-jazz steps. Today, the disco is more electro but retains its cool alternative identity, hosting notably the decadent House of Moda parties. These wild queer nights are the best, with fabulous disco tunes, fun vibes, and a dash of diva dazzle. The exciting Exotica parties, helmed by the funky DJ collective Les Yeux Orange, are also excellent.

🎯 Thu-Sat 12am-6am   📞 +33 1 42 02 20 52   💲 Free

© Cédric Canezza

LE BUS PALLADIUM

6, rue Fontaine (9th) Ⓜ Pigalle

📷 @lebuspalladium

The Parisian temple of rock, Le Bus dates back to the 60's. Dali and Jagger partied here, while French rock stars cut their teeth on the stage. This aura of legend still float around. Down in the intimate stage room, freak out to rowdy live gigs and pulsating Twist and Shout parties. But the upstairs bar is the place. It's more chill and cosy, yet always great fun. Le Bus is a small, intimate space, so it can play hard to get. The best way to get in is pulling out your inner rock self.

🎯 Tue from 8pm live +dj   📞 +33 1 45 26 80 35   💲 €20 cover (two drinks)
    Thu-Sat 9pm-6am (gig till 12:30, then club)

PARTY JOINTS -EDGY & GRITTY-

© La Machine

LA MACHINE DU MOULIN ROUGE (LA CHAUFFERIE)
90, bd de Clichy (18th) (M) Blanche

(O) @lamachineparis

Under the famous Moulin Rouge, thrives a club. This former rock haunt that hosted Elvis and Bowie in the 80's has been given a second wind. Sure, there is the main dancefloor (le Central) and the chill rooftop, but the best bit is the intimate room in the basement, la Chaufferie ("boiler room"), for it was the cabaret's real boiler room. The space fits 400 dancers and acts as a lab for emerging European talents. The expert line-up spreads across gabber, jungle, bass, tech-house, and minimal, featuring all the cool Parisian underground collectives.

(K) Fri-Sat 12pm-6am

(C) +33 1 53 41 88 89   (S) €9-16

@freerubens

NUITS FAUVES
34, quai d'Austerlitz (12th) (M) Gare d'Austerlitz

(O) @nuitsfauvesparis

Under the decks of the big green ship positioned on the banks of the Seine – the Fashion & Design Institute – lies a warehouse club that has plenty of power under the hood. The edgy minimalist décor and the sick lighting set-up are the backdrop for tech-house wild nights ("nuits fauves"), with heavyweights such as Brodisnki, Shølmo, Recondite, or Kenny Dope gracing the stage. Recently made XXL by merging with its sister venue on the top floor, the huge raw space is now the biggest party playground in town.

(K) Fri-Sat 11pm-6am   (S) €12-17

© Come Cerezo

LA STATION GARE DES MINES
29, avenue de la Porte d'Aubervilliers (18th)
(M) Porte de la Chapelle

(O) @collectifnu

The ultimate underground party spot, La Station has settled in shut down train tracks, at the edge of inner-city Paris. Cross the ring road and you will arrive at a wasteland. There, you'll find pallets and containers serving as a bar, a superb sound system, and a huge outdoor dancefloor in the wilderness. The expert line-up ranges from raging rock to thunderous techno. Seedy industrial setting and low-key crowd – it feels like Berlin, before Berlin was even hip.

 Note to self: From Porte d'Aubervilliers, after crossing the ringroad, follow the red signs (Raboni & Loxam) and take the path on your left.

(K) Fri-Sat 10pm-6am   (S) €7-10

© L'Aérosol

L'AÉROSOL
54, rue de l'Évangile (18th) Ⓜ Porte de la Chapelle

📷 @laerosol_paris

The first Parisian spot dedicated to street art, L'Aérosol camps in an abandoned rail warehouse. Originally a one-off thing, it was such a hit that the adventure continued. You can drop by this unique museum, check out the work of local street-artists on the Wall of Fame, buy gear at the on-site shop and try your hand at graffing, ride, or just chill on the gigantic terrace lined with food trucks. But it's also a super party spot! Their clubbing roller is the bee's knees, with a dope line-up, sweetly tasting of tech-house, minimal, and disco.

🎟 Wed-Sun 11am-9pm / Closed on Mon & Tue ☎ +33 1 34 18 86 83 💲 Free

© Gaetan Tracqui

LA CLAIRIÈRE
1, carrefour de Longchamp (16th) Ⓜ Porte Maillot

📷 @la.clairiere

The wide-open spaces of the Bois de Boulogne forest are a sweet playground for alfresco fiestas. This ephemeral summer club, first set up in 2016, has now taken permanent residence right by the Longchamp racecourse. Nestled in a lush green setting, the preserved place is handled by the GoodPlanet foundation, which throws a series of parties for good causes. For a stellar gig under the stars, venture towards the western side of town. The line-up is worth the trip and organic food trucks to boot.

💡 **Note to self:** Bus 244 from Porte Maillot till 12:30am.

🎟 Fri-Sat 10pm-5am 💲 €20-30

RELAX

TAKE CARE

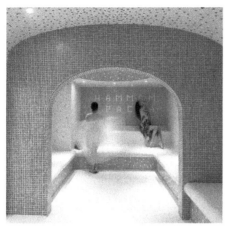

HAMMAM PACHA
17, rue Mayet (6th) Ⓜ Duroc

Ⓞ @hammampacha_officiel

Hammam is a tradition the French happily borrowed from the Moroccan community. The ritual includes basking in a steam room on a warm stone, dipping in the Jacuzzi, and smearing yourself in soft black soap for a killer scrub that'll leave your skin feeling soft as silk. Then head down to the lounge, an oriental boudoir, for a mint tea and delish pastries. You can while away hours here without realising. The Pacha is spick and span; your safest bet! Women only.

🔆 **Note to self:** For an even more relaxing time, avoid the crowds, go on weekdays.

⊛ Mon-Wed 11am-7pm / Thu- Fri 11am-10pm
Sat- Sun 10am-7pm

Ⓒ +33 1 43 06 55 55   Ⓢ Dive

SPA BY CLARINS
8, avenue de la Porte Molitor (16th) Ⓜ Michel-Ange - Molitor

Ⓞ @mltrparis

The historic Molitor swimming pool houses within its mustard walls the biggest spa in town. Sprawling across an entire floor, the stylish retro space boasts of 13 cabins and a fresh mood that will transport you. Dive into the signature Beyond the Water treatment, specially devised by Clarins. After relaxing to watery sounds, let your body float under aquatic cushions for a massage with this weightless blissful feel. Coming to the Molitor is a bit of a treat anyway, so get the whole package, which will grant you access to the exclusive pool. Besides an exorbitant membership or a stay at the MGallery hotel (see p.124), it's your only way in to the stunning Art Deco pool.

⊛ Mon-Sun 10am-8pm   Ⓒ +33 1 56 07 08 50   Ⓢ Casual Chic

SPA NUXE

32-34, rue Montorgueil (1st) Ⓜ Etienne Marcel

📷 @nuxefrance

Under the stoned vaults and timber ceiling of a 17th-century wine cellar, breathes an enchanting place. Converted into a spa by the nature brand NUXE, the historic building is a sanctuary where time stands still. In case you're not too familiar with NUXE, let's just say it is France's best-loved pharmacy brand, famous for its natural remedies. Indulge in a massage with the house's star Huile Prodigieuse – their magical must-have, a multi-purpose dry oil that smells like heavenly warm sand.

🕓 Mon-Fri 10am-9pm / Sat 9:30am-7:30pm
Sun 11am-12:45 & 1:45pm-7pm

📞 +33 1 42 36 65 65   💲 Casual Chic

© Vincent Leroux

SPA CHANEL AT THE RITZ

Le Ritz Club 17, place Vendôme (1st) Ⓜ Concorde

📷 @ritzparis

Chanel and the Ritz share history. Coco was a regular of the palace, where she even settled for many years. Honouring this memory and the spirit of the two maisons, this exceptional spa is an ode to discrete refinement. Minimalist and elegant, the alcoves are inspired from Mademoiselle's apartments. Using exclusively-created products, the couture treatments will leave you feeling rejuvenated. It's a special indulgence of course, but it's much more than a simple facial we are talking here; a complete experience, rather, with cocktails concocted by the house star mixologist, the same silk linen as Mrs Chanel, and other delicate details. Basically, luxury in its simplest attire.

🕓 Mon-Sun 10am-9pm   📞 +33 1 43 16 30 60   💲 Fancy Pants

GO GREEN

JARDIN DU LUXEMBOURG
(6th) Ⓜ Saint-Sulpice

Half French, half English, in formal style, but quintessentially Parisian at heart, this garden nestled in the Latin Quarter is an enchanting place. Brimming with *joie de vivre,* the park is filled with readers, lovers, Sorbonne students, old folks playing chess, and kids sailing vintage boats in the central pond. The vast green space houses multiple settings: lively playgrounds, intimate nooks, and crannies, picturesque bandstands, orchid glasshouses, a rose garden, an orange grove, and what not. It's also an open-air museum, dotted with a hundred statues, and the beautiful Medicis fountain which takes centre stage.

🕐 Mon-Sun 8am-5/6pm (winter) 8/9pm (summer)   💲 Free

JARDIN DES TUILERIES
(1st) Ⓜ Tuileries

With the Louvre at one end and the Concorde plaza on the other, this garden enjoys a royal position. André Le Nôtre, Versailles' landscape architect, made it a proper *jardin à la française* (French formal garden) in 1664 – geometric flowerbeds, linear perspectives, and an impeccable square trim. The two ponds are the meeting place for kids who, like in old times, sail wooden toy boats. Grab one of the iconic green garden chairs to lounge in the sun! Or stroll and spot statues by Maillol, Rodin, Dubuffet, and Giacometti running along the alleys of lime trees.

🕐 Mon-Sun 7:30am-9pm   💲 Free
(7:30pm in winter, 11pm in summer)

LA COULÉE VERTE
(12th) Ⓜ Bastille

Enjoy a bucolic trail without leaving the city centre! This old railway track converted into a pedestrian walk will take you through tunnels, suspension bridges, and hidden gardens. Standing seven meters above street level, the 5-kilometer path overlooks the city. But the aptly named green track ("coulée verte") is first and foremost a lush nature destination.
Access through Viaduc des Arts (from Bastille opera, take rue de Lyon; then the staircase on your left, next to the car park, will lead you to the viaduct)

JARDIN DES PLANTES
(5th) (M) Gare d'Austerlitz

(O) @le_museum

An oasis in the midst of urban land, the botanical and zoological garden is an exotic place that combines nature, architecture, and history. The neat central perspective, sheltered alleys, romantic rose garden, art deco greenhouses, and wild alpine garden are the many green spaces to explore. With its 1200 animals, the menagerie is much loved by kids. Opened in 1794, it's one of the oldest zoos in the world. Aiming to reconnect the urban audience with nature, the passionate team organises urban biodiversity walks and workshops regularly.

(K) Mon-Sun 7:30am-8pm   (S) Free / Zoo €10-13

@aliciatreguer

© Marc Bertrand - Paris Tourist Office

PARC DES BUTTES CHAUMONT
(19th) (M) Buttes Chaumont

(O) @parclesbutteschaumont

Set up on former quarries, this leafy park has retained a few hills, that will take you 40 meters above ground, and treat you to clear views of Paris. One of the prettiest green spots in town, it's filled with wonders to explore: caves, a waterfall, a suspension walkaway, and even a temple perched atop a steep island. Climb up to the belvedere, and you'll be rewarded with a panoramic view of Montmartre. For a rustic fiesta, swing by the Pavillon Puebla. This *guinguette* is a lovely haven to chill over rosé wine.

(K) Mon-Sun 7am-9pm   (S) Free

GO GREEN

BOIS DE BOULOGNE
(16th) (M) Rue de la Pompe

Cycling, horse-riding, running, strolling, boating, there are many ways to explore the huge forest spread on the south-western edge of Paris. The dream spot for a picnic or a day off with the nature, it can invigorate souls. It's also packed with options for the more restless. Hike to the waterfall (Grande Cascade) and explore the two hidden caves, visit Marie Antoinette's greenhouses (Serres d'Auteuil), or reconnect with your inner kid and fool around in the retro amusement park (the Jardin d'Acclimatation, which was opened in 1860 by Napoleon).

PÈRE LACHAISE
8, boulevard de Ménilmontant (20th) (M) Philippe Auguste

Looking for some quiet? There is no better place! Remotely located in the East of Paris, this huge cemetery is the last home of many famous residents. A great number of French legends rest here, whether writers, painters, musicians, film folks, or politicians. Along the leafy alleys, find curiosities of all kinds. Look out for Oscar Wilde's outrageous grave, which had to be protected from lipstick marks, or for Jim Morrison's tomb littered with whisky flasks, cigarette butts, and poems. Read the silence and you'll find a bit of history, art, culture and nature altogether. A peaceful walk down memory lane.

 Mon-Sun 8am-6pm   (S) Free

© Marc Bertrand / Paris Tourist Office

ALONG THE CANALS...
(10th & 19th) (M) République

Its locks and green metal turning bridges make the Canal Saint-Martin a charming retreat for a quick fix of nature within the inner-city reach. A short hop from République, you will land up in a half-pedestrian haven. Under lush trees, follow the cobbled quaysides dotted with quirky boutiques and cute eateries. A bicycle path runs alongside the water, or you can boat (then, you even get to see the underground bit of the canal, under the Bastille square). The ramble stretches over 6 km and ends at La Villette Lake, where more fun things await.

HOP ON THE ISLANDS!
(1st & 4th) (M) Pont Neuf

The heart of Paris, geographically and historically, the Cité is not only home to the Notre-Dame, but also the Conciergerie, a gothic prison. At the tip of the island (Pont Neuf), go down to the banks, at the centre of the bridge, behind the statue. The Square du Vert-Galant nestled here is a sweet spot! Check out Au Vieux Paris d'Arcole, an adorable eatery whose lilac-covered facade is Instagram-worthy.

The muted atmosphere of the Saint-Louis Island will offer a contrast. Almost entirely filled with private mansions and age-old gourmet shops, the place is untouched by urban frenzy. Don't miss the panorama from the bridges!

LE QUARTIER SPORT
17, rue de Pontoise (5th) Ⓜ Maubert Mutualité

Just as majestic as its famous sister The Molitor (see p.124) but way more accessible, this gem of a pool is a best-kept secret. Erected in 1933, the Art Deco building stands, unaffected by age. With its charming old-school cabins and symmetric passageways, it's one of the most soothing spots for a swim in Paris. Visit after sunset on weekdays (the pool stays open till midnight) for a one-of-a-kind swimming experience. Doing laps to classical music, with a rainbow-lit architectural backdrop is indeed magical.

🕐 Mon-Fri 7am-8:30am & 12:15pm-1:30pm & 4:30pm-12am
Wed 7am-8:30am & 11:30am-7:30pm & 8:15pm-12am
Sat 10am-7pm / Sun 8am-7pm
Closed on Tue & Thu 7pm-8:15pm

💲 €4.80, €43 for 10
€11/night entry

GET PHYSICAL

SAILING ON CANAL DE L'OURCQ

HOOP TONIC
© Giada Aline

SAILING ON CANAL DE L'OURCQ

37, quai de la Seine (19th) Ⓜ Riquet

📷 @marindeaudoucefrance

Rent your own boat and explore yet another side of Paris! They are electrical boats, so green and easy-peasy navigation (no license required, you can be the captain!). The crew is top class; they provide mulled wine and blankets when it's chilly outside and even prepare you *apéro* baskets (on demand). The two-hour cruise makes for a pleasant sail across the Canal de l'Ourcq. If you wish to push it towards Canal Saint Martin, get down into its locks and tunnels, check out the options; it's much more intimate than the big tourist boats! For 5 to 11 sailors.

🎟 Mon-Sun 9:30am-10pm

📞 +33 1 42 09 54 10   💲 €13-14 / head for 2h

URBAN CHALLENGE

📷 @urbanchallenge

Tired of your treadmill routine? Join this intensive open-air workout! The killer program, mixing running and bodybuilding, brings out your very best. The natural setting, teammates, and extra-ordinary instructors (firemen, athletes) are seriously stimulating. Every day, no matter the weather, evening and lunchtime sessions are held in a dozen Parisian parks (Buttes Chaumont, Luxembourg, Tuileries...).
Book on www.urban-challenge.fr

💲 €15 / session, €89 / 10 sessions (first class free)

HOOP TONIC

📷 @hoop_tonic

Got fond memories of the 80's hula-hoop craze? Pull out your retro workout apparels and come wiggle on the fitness mode! It's so much fun to not drag your feet to the gym for a change. But don't think that it's just a kiddie game! Burning 600 calories an hour, the HoopTonic will definitely make your muscles stronger. The cardio-cum-core combo is badass. Plus, yes, sure thing, all that hip rolling will bring the sexy back. Locations in the 3rd, 8th, 9th & 10th districts.
Check out class details and book online at www.hooptonic.net

💲 €15 / class

PÉTANQUE

BALLERINA YOGA

BOATING IN BOIS DE BOULOGNE

BALLERINA YOGA

10, rue Volney (2nd) Ⓜ Opéra

Ⓞ @elephantpaname

Where sports meet art and spirituality; this new activity bridges the mini gap between yoga and ballet, two disciplines that require agility, flexibility, and balance. Adding grace to the mix and a dose of gentleness to the usually strict ballet technics, this hybrid works like a charm. Carole, yogi and dancer at the Opera, guides you through a holistic two-hour workshop connecting the body and mind.
Book on www.carolemelosi.com

Ⓒ +33 1 49 27 83 33   Ⓢ €40 / workshop

PÉTANQUE

Quintessentially French, this folk game is a must! Mostly played in the South, *pétanque* is all about summer, friends, and rosé wine. In a dozen green spots, find strips of free access (the quaint Place Dauphine on the Cité Island, the chic Palais Royal, or the atypical Arènes de Lutèce – a Roman amphitheater). Or, in case you don't own the gear, head down to **Bar Ourcq** on the Canal. This chill bar lends boules for free, so on sunny evenings, you'll always find playmates! The other go-to is the southern joint **Les Nicois** (see p.98) who even designed their own boules.

BOATING IN BOIS DE BOULOGNE

Châlet des Îles, Chemin de Ceinture du Lac Inférieur, Porte de la Muette (16th) Ⓜ Rue de la Pompe

Whether as the ultimate romantic thing, or simply a relaxing bucolic activity, boating in the Bois will enchant you. Explore the two islands, spot fishes and turtles, listen to the chirping birds and lapping water, stop for a beer under the weeping willow. Don't underestimate the sporting side though, so bring along a strong rower!

Ⓚ Mon-Sun 12pm-6pm   Ⓢ €12 / hour
(from mid-March to late Oct.)

HÔTEL EDGAR
© Thomas Millet

SLEEP

SLEEP

THE HOXTON
30-32, rue du Sentier (2nd) Ⓜ Bonne Nouvelle

 @thehoxtonhotel

'The Hox' is the coolest kid on the block. After earning its stripes in Shoreditch and Williamsburg, the edgy group took this historic mansion over with their signature dose of designer flair. With two picturesque courtyards, preserved heritage, an exotic bar and exciting interiors, it's the real deal. It's all been kept simple (no mini bar, slippers or unnecessary extras), so it stays easy on the pocket. Oh, and guess what? Breakfast comes in a bag delivered at your doorstep so you can laze in bed.

Ⓒ +33 1 85 65 75 00 　　　　Ⓢ Dive

© Thomas Millet

HÔTEL EDGAR
30-32, rue du Sentier (2nd) Ⓜ Bonne Nouvelle

Ⓞ @hotel_edgar

Edgar is true art; and that's no exaggeration! Each of the twelve rooms has a one-of-a-kind mood, designed by an artist. This quirky place, once a clothing workshop, oozes style and personality. Its interiors will knock you off your socks. Don't fear, though. The design doesn't come with an attitude. The Edgar team are just adorable! The hotel is nestled in a quiet corner of an edgy neighbourhood, but the restaurant is always packed. A spot for the cool cats that like to stray from the beaten track.

Ⓒ +33 1 40 41 05 19　　　　Ⓢ Casual Chic

AUBERGE FLORA
44, bd Richard Lenoir (11th) (M) Richard Lenoir

(O) @mikula_flora

Flora Mikula, seasoned chef, welcomes you in her little boutique auberge (inn), matched by her brilliant restaurant. This modern-day inn is a cosy, straightforward spot with 31 stylish rooms, which feels just like home. Perfectly located at the heart of the bustling Bastille-Oberkampf district, the place is just a short walk from the Marais. It's compact yet comfy, no-frills but irresistible. The restaurant is a must; you'll get treated to a hearty breakfast, top-notch tapas or other zesty dishes, all infused with Flora's flair and Mediterranean touch.

(C) +33 147 00 52 77   (S) Dive

GRAND PIGALLE HOTEL
29, rue Victor Massé (9th) (M) Pigalle

(O) @grandpigallehotel

Brainchild of the excellent Experimental Group (who also boast a couple of stellar speakeasies and hip eateries), this retro chic hotel is ideally positioned, in buzzing SoPi. You'll be surrounded by a sea of bars, restaurants, cafes, bakeries, cellars and what not. In a local and authentic neighbourhood, only at a stone's throw from all the main attractions, this super central pied-à-terre is perfect to live à la parisienne. The restaurant is top-notch.

-:O:- Note to self: For sweet craves and breaky on the go, the bakery next door is fab!

(C) +33 1 85 73 12 00   (S) Casual Chic

SLEEP

LE CITIZEN HOTEL

96, quai de Jemmapes (10th) Ⓜ Jacques Bonsergent

📷 @lecitizenhotel

Sitting on the cobbled quays of the canal Saint-Martin, this eco-friendly hotel is a zen oasis in a buzzing neighborhood. Fully handcrafted with natural wood, the interiors have a rustic, minimalistic charm. This intimate address (12 rooms only) feels more like a guesthouse, really. Cool addition: it's a super family-friendly spot! The top floors and rooms connect to form an apartment. The breakfast is fresh and free; and there is also a Japanese canteen.

☎ +33 1 83 62 55 50   💲 Casual Chic

© Joyce Attali   © Frédéric Baron-Morin

MGALLERY BY SOFITEL MOLITOR

13, rue Nungesser et Coli (16th) Ⓜ Michel-Ange - Molitor

📷 @mltrparis

This iconic mustard-yellow pool is legendary. « The Molitor » is where the bikini made its debut in the 1940's. Parisian it-girls of the time would hang out and sunbathe here. Changing cubicles were converted into spacious, stylish rooms, giving the Art Deco pool complex a second life. The Sofitel venue also flaunts a massive spa (the biggest in Europe) and a stunning rooftop with an Eiffel Tower view. If you feel like escaping the hustle and bustle to lounge by the pool, this is your haven! Not going to lie, it's not bang in the city centre (just a metro ride away, though), but nestled in chic south-western Paris – next-door to the Roland Garros courts.

☎ +33 1 56 07 08 50   💲 Fancy Pants

ESCAPE

© Eric Sander

GIVERNY

 @fondationmonet

This tiny Seine-side village is globally famous. Does it ring a bell? Giverny was the hotspot of Impressionism, since it's where Claude Monet lived, loved, worked, and drew inspiration from. Remember the famous water lilies series? That's Giverny! Step into the picturesque landscapes immortalised by Impressionist masterpieces. Soak in the dreamy atmosphere. You can visit the artist's house and gardens, whose foliage and vivid colours make for a bucolic stroll.

Do not miss: The famous bridge over the picture-perfect water-lily ponds in the garden. Savour an alfresco lunch at one of the nearby cafes, the village is full of them!

Getting there:

🚗 1h on the A13 highway

🚆 45 minutes from Paris Saint-Lazare station to Vernon; then a shuttle bus will take you to Giverny (total €15, one way)

💡 **Note to self:** The gardens are open from late March to November 1rst. Ensure you arrive early and pre-book tickets to avoid the crowds.

🕐 Mon-Sun 9:30am-5:30pm   💲 €9.50

© Eric Sander

VERSAILLES

@chateauversailles

Its very name is synonymous with grandeur and evocative of outrageous extravagance. Dive into the golden age of French history and bring back to life the Sun's King, Marie Antoinette, and other legends from the times. Honestly, it's gigantic (get a map, as you can easily get lost among the 2300 rooms), so you'll need time – at least half a day. The palace is sublime of course, but the gardens are otherworldly beautiful. So, try to visit on a rain-free day and spend time there!

Heads-up, Versailles is Versailles, so there'll always be a long line. Pre-book tickets, arrive early, but be prepared for a wait anyway. The smart thing would be to visit the gardens first, then heading to the palace post lunch to avoid the morning crowd. An even better option would be to spend a few extra bucks on the guided tour. This will allow you to skip the lines, get insightful historical info that will enhance your visit, and also access some restricted places.

Do not miss: The Hall of Mirrors, a must-see that lives to its reputation and makes heads spin. If time and weather allows, head to the Grand Trianon and Marie Antoinette's domain (the Queen's Hamlet). In order to get away from the mundane matters of the court, the queen had arranged her pad in the park, resembling a countryside estate. A world away from the palace's gilt and extravaganza, it's a real hidden gem!

Getting there:

🚇 30-40 minutes by the commuter train RER C to Versailles-Rive Gauche station.

🕐 Tue-Sun 9am-6pm (park 7am-8:30pm) / Closed on Mon   💲 €18-20

VERSAILLES
@amauryzep

DEAUVILLE
© Béatrice Augier

DEAUVILLE

@deauvilleofficial

Ditch the city and head to Normandy! The closest seaside resort to the capital, Deauville is the Parisian equivalent of the Hamptons. Not only does the "Parisian Riviera" have its share of marinas, swanky villas and hotels, golf and horseracing courses, but it's also the perfect romantic getaway! Its distinctive colourful parasols, cinematic promenade, the Grand Casino, and American film festival give Deauville its panache. Perfect for a weekend trip, the town and its famous beach are a charming retreat.

Do not miss: Les Planches, the iconic promenade where wooden bathing cabins are dedicated to famous film stars that have attended the festival.

Getting there:

🚗 2h30 on the A13 highway

🚆 2h30 from Saint-Lazare station (€15–35)

ESCAPE

DISNEYLAND PARIS

DISNEYLAND PARIS

@ @disneylandparis

Pause reality for one day and step into the wonder world of Disney. Truth be told, it's much more than just a theme park. When the animated companions of your childhood come to life, it's a lot like magic! There is something for everyone in this gigantic playground: big thrills rides, enchanting encounters, spectacular shows, some seriously awesome attractions and geeky stuff (one word: Star Wars). Awaken your inner child and dive right in! Around for Christmas or Halloween? Don't miss it, because it's twice more fun!

Do not miss: The Tower of Terror and Rock 'n' Roller Coaster for the adrenaline-junkies. It's a Small World, Big Thunder Mountain, and Pirates of the Caribbean for milder adventures. Oh, and you must catch the parade and the illuminations: it's absolutely wowing!

Getting there:

🚇 40 minutes with RER (Regional Express Railway) A to Marne la Vallée

💲 €42-79 / one-day pass

MONT ST-MICHEL

@ @montsaintmichel_normandie

Emerging as an oasis amidst a desert of mudflats, this magical island is one of the most stunning sights you'll see in France (maybe even Europe). The surreal stretch of land houses a medieval town protected by ramparts and crowned by a gravity-defying abbey. This holy mount also boasts some of the biggest tidal variations in the world – the waters can withdraw as far as 15km from the shore! Cross the bay on foot during low tide, and you'll be able to observe the ever-changing nature, light and reflections.

Do not miss: The lookout points and their unrivalled views of the bay. Climb up the 350 steps to the abbey to see its cloister and the Marvel, the glorious gothic chambers that cling spectacularly to the rock.

Getting there:

🚗 4h30 via A13 or A11/A81

🚆 4h from Paris Montparnasse to Villedieu-les-Poêles station, then shuttle (€27)

💡 **Note to self:** The car park is located 2.4 km away from the island to preserve the shoreline. Head to Place des Navettes, where free shuttle buses called Passeurs will take you to the mount. You can also book a Maringote, a special horse-drawn carriage (€5.30/head).

🕐 Mon-Sun 9am-6/7pm   💲 €10

MONT ST-MICHEL

LYON
© Tristan Deschamps

LYON

📷 @villedelyon

Sitting strategically where the Saône meets the Rhône, France's third largest city has been a major hub since the Roman times. Lyon indeed has 2,000 years of history to tell and a lot more up its sleeve. A walk through Vieux Lyon cobblestone streets will arouse your curiosity. The medieval Renaissance neighbourhood is filled with wonders to discover. Look out for *traboules,* the secret passages that connect streets through buildings underground. The panorama from the top of the basilica is worth the trip up the Fourvière hill, especially by cable car.

Do not miss: The food! It's hearty, rib-sticking, mostly carnivorous, and a little old school, but if you're an adventurous gourmet, you'll love it! Else, there is always the *cervelle de canuts* (a cottage cheese based specialty) and the pink praline tart. In any case, a meal in a *bouchon* is part and parcel of the Lyon experience.

If you have the time, also drop by the **Musée des Confluences.** Its stunning sustainable design and eclectic collections, ranging from natural history to anthropology, across arts and world civilizations, are worth the go! Party-wise, if you're around for **Nuit Sonores** or **La Chinerie Festival,** check out their superb line-up! Otherwise, head to **Le Sucre.** This warehouse rooftop hosts top flight electro gigs and cool events.

Getting there:

🚗 5h drive on the A6 highway

🚆 2h by TGV (superfast train) from Paris Gare de Lyon to Lyon Part-Dieu

TRAVEL JOURNAL

PLACE: WEATHER: DATE:

PLACE: WEATHER: DATE:

TRAVEL JOURNAL

PLACE: _____ WEATHER: _____ DATE: _____

TRAVEL JOURNAL

PLACE: WEATHER: DATE:

TRAVEL JOURNAL

PLACE: _____   WEATHER: _____   DATE: _____

TRAVEL JOURNAL

PLACE: _____   WEATHER: _____   DATE: _____

Didi & Co
TRAVEL GUIDE

www.didiandcotravel.com

Concept & Words
Caroline & Geraldine Boyer

Graphic Magic
Squid Creative Team

Printed By
IngramSpark

MONEY MEMO 💲
Eat
Dive > €15
Casual Chic €15-40
Fancy Pants €40+
(average meal, per head)

Sleep
Dive < $€100
Casual Chic €100-200
Fancy Pants €200+
(one night, per head)

SPECIAL ⭕ SHOUT-OUT TO...
Local Legends
Giulietta Canzani Mora
Victor Lugger
Marie Mautalen
Solène Miroglio
Nicholle Kobi
Alicia Tréguer

Parisian Folks
Benjamin Boyer
Victor de Broca
Amandine Carle
Flora Coppolani
Chris Cottard
Pierre-Alexis Hermet
Warren Ichou
Marion Innocenzi
Barbara Jacquin
Adèle Lanson
Maelle Olivier
Margot Paquien
Simon Robert
(foodwineandstyle)
Kim Sentis
Louise Van den Bogaert,
as well as all the companies and organizations for your invaluable input, steady support and happy vibes!

Local Eyes
Amaury (@amauryzep)
Arjun (@arjunradhakrishnan)
Bianca (@foodwithlegs)
ChopChicks in Paris:
Diana, Jocelyn & Melissa
(@chopchicksinparis)
Dana (@danaberez)
Kathy (@foodloversodyssey)
Lucia (@luciatalkspictures)
Mathieu (Gavroche Père & Fils)
Morgan (@morganabbou)
Stéphanie (@dkomag)
Vincent (@vm.parisphoto)
Willem (@freeaparis),
as well as the Paris Tourist Office, Free Rubens, Gaëtan Tracqui and all the pros behind the photos.

Didi & Co Sas
1600B, Chemin de Belle Eau
26780 Malataverne, France.

Content is compiled based on info available as of March 2018. Please don't blame the messenger if some bits (the chef, the menu, the rates) changed between our going to press and your visit.

ISBN 979-10-97530-02-0
Dépôt légal: May 2018

136

CPSIA information can be obtained
at www.ICGtesting.com
Printed in the USA
LVHW07s1501020918
588935LV00020B/106/P